FIXING FARM TRADE

THE COUNCIL ON FOREIGN RELATIONS SERIES
ON INTERNATIONAL TRADE

C. Michael Aho, Editor

FIXING FARM TRADE
Policy Options for the United States

ROBERT L. PAARLBERG

BALLINGER PUBLISHING COMPANY
Cambridge, Massachusetts
A Subsidiary of Harper & Row, Publishers, Inc.

International Standard Book Number: 0-88730-196-7

Library of Congress Catalog Card Number: 87-24118

Printed in the United States of America

Library of Congress Cataloging-in-Publication Data

Paarlberg, Robert L.
  Fixing farm trade.

  (The Council on Foreign Relations series on international trade)
  "A Council on Foreign Relations book."
  Includes index.
  1. Produce trade–Government policy–United States.
2. Agriculture and states–United States. 3. United
States–Commercial policy. 4. Agriculture–Economic
aspects–United States. I. Title. II. Series.
HD9006.P27 1987   382'.41'0973   87-24118
ISBN 0-88730-196-7

Contents

v

List of Tables and Figures

Foreword

C. Michael Aho

The situation concerning trade in agriculture is both tragic and absurd. It is tragic because at the same time that we have mountains of surplus butter and seas of excess grain, millions of people are starving. It is absurd because agricultural programs are already costing billions of dollars annually (often paid to well-to-do farmers), and now countries are getting into an export subsidy war to see who can sell more cheaply to the Soviet Union. The Uruguay Round of multilateral trade negotiations, launched in September 1986, provides an opportunity to address these issues, but it will not be enough.

Rob Paarlberg, in this cogent, well-argued book, describes the nature of the agricultural trade problems that threaten to break out into wider trade wars, and lays out an agenda for solving those problems. Paarlberg does this not solely from the perspective of an agricultural expert (he is that), or of an optimistic trade specialist who expects the Uruguay Round to solve all of our problems. His analysis and recommendations are based upon rigorous academic studies and upon knowledge of the hard realities of politics in agriculture. In the process of writing this book, his analysis has withstood the test of agricultural experts, agricultural interests and trade specialists. None of them agrees with all of his recommendations, but they do agree on the depth and insightfulness of his analysis.

Agriculture has been an exception in past trade negotiations, and has almost stood in the way of agreements in other areas. Agriculture's exceptional status is apparent in many ways: 1)

Agriculture is the only trade sector headed by a cabinet ministry and staffed by a large bureaucracy; 2) national legislatures in several countries give a disproportionate share of the legislature to the rural, agricultural producing areas; 3) farm groups are well-organized and have years of experience in lobbying activity; and, as a result, 4) national legislation and international agreements have historically treated agriculture differently from industry.

Why tackle agriculture now? At least four reasons come to mind: 1) Budgetary overruns are occurring at a time when budget deficits are a source of concern in most countries; 2) a group of fair traders in agriculture (the Cairns Group) has emerged which is putting pressure on the European Community and the United States, the two biggest offenders; 3) lack of discipline in agriculture undermines confidence in the rules of the trading system, and disputes threaten to spill over to trade in industrial products; and 4) agriculture is becoming a major foreign policy issue.

In short, agriculture is becoming too important to leave to agricultural ministers. Finance, trade and foreign ministers must get involved, and maybe even heads of state. The Uruguay Round provides one such opportunity, and the discussions at the last two Economic Summits have been another. But trade negotiations are as much domestic negotiations as they are negotiations among countries. At a national level, a countervailing force of consumers, industrialists and retailers must be mobilized in order to amend the national legislation that lies at the heart of agricultural trade problems.

This book clearly and concisely lays out what must be done at both a national and an international level if the trade problems in agriculture are going to be resolved. It is a timely book because if nations do not begin to cooperate in agricultural trade issues, we risk unilateral responses that could fragment the entire trading system.

Fixing Farm Trade is the first in a series of books on trade issues that will be produced by the Council on Foreign Relations' International Trade Project. I cannot think of a better book to begin with. Future volumes will focus upon international corporate alliances, the developing countries in the trading system, the U.S. domestic politics of trade, trade problems in high-technology industries, the U.S.-Canadian bilateral trade talks, and the future of U.S. trade policy, among others. In all, the Project will produce 10-12 monographs over the next two years. These monographs will be based upon a series of Council study groups.

On behalf of the Council, I would like to thank General Motors and the Rockefeller Foundation for their generous funding of the project, as well as the AMAX Foundation which provided funds—in honor of Walter B. Hochschild—to support a review of the monograph's early draft. I would personally like to thank Joseph Greenwald who so ably chaired the study group, and the members of the Project's Steering Committee (see Appendix) chaired so ably by Edmund T. Pratt Jr. I would also like to thank Peter Tarnoff, President of the Council, and Paul Kreisberg, Director of Studies, for their unwavering support. Finally, a word of appreciation for Rob Paarlberg who not only produced a first-rate book, but who also delivered it ahead of schedule. Editors everywhere wish that all authors were so punctual and responsible.

C. Michael Aho is Director of the International Trade Project, and Senior Fellow for Economics at the Council on Foreign Relations.

Preface

This book is the first in a series on present day international trade policy issues that is being published under the auspices of the Council on Foreign Relations in New York city. Why should such a series begin with a book devoted just to agriculture? Trade policy officials, who have seen agricultural disputes move to center stage at economic summit meetings and in the current Uruguay Round of GATT negotiations, will have no trouble understanding this choice. Nor will most academic specialists, who point with alarm to the high levels of distortion and disruption in today's international agricultural markets. Budget officials who have long bemoaned the high cost of domestic farm subsidy programs, and must now absorb the growing cost of agricultural export subsidies as well, will also appreciate this choice. So will diplomats who must manage the tensions and respond to the harsh foreign criticisms generated by those subsidies. Most interested of all should be U.S. agricultural producers, who have seen the value of their export sales fall, despite subsidies, by a disastrous 40 percent thus far in the 1980s. For all of these interested and affected parties, fixing farm trade is a high priority.

I agreed to write this book on agricultural trade issues for the Council on Foreign Relations after getting two assurances. The first was a guarantee that my work would be subject, before publication, to the scrutiny and criticism of a wide range of senior agricultural policy specialists. For this purpose the Council allowed me to present several draft chapters of this manuscript to a study group on agricultural trade policy, which I directed, that met four times in 1986 in Washington, D.C., and New York. The members of this study group included past and present senior practitioners in agricultural and trade policy, both from the United States and from abroad, foreign policy specialists, policy advocates and senior operators from production agriculture and agribusiness, elected representatives from farm states and their staff, and agricultural policy analysts from the academic and research community. (For a list of the study group members, see Appendix.) The deliberations of this study group began with the review of four separately authored discussion papers—which helped to inform my own thinking and which laid a firm foundation for my subsequent drafts—that were presented in turn to the group for discussion and criticism. Every author knows the value of receiving early and vigorous criticism from a lively and diverse audience. Without the high-quality feedback that was made available to me in this fashion, my efforts would have moved more slowly and would have produced, I am sure, a less satisfying result.

The second important assurance given to me by the Council was that this book would be, in the end, entirely my own. I wanted the benefit of probing criticism and informed advice, but not at the cost of removing all the sharp edges from my own argument. I did not want to feel obliged to give equal weight to all the different viewpoints expressed by my critics, nor did I want to have to produce a "consensus document" bland enough for everyone to support. I wanted the disputatious nature of agricultural trade policy to remain visible in my work. As an independent scholar with no record of prior government service to defend, no particular institutional or political interest to promote, and no commercial constituency to serve, I have always been most comfortable speaking only for myself, and letting the chips fall where they may. I thank the Council for allowing me, with its support, the luxury of this approach.

I have received so much helpful advice and assistance in drafting this book that it will be impossible to discharge here my full debt of gratitude. I must begin by thanking Joseph A. Greenwald, my study group Chairman, who ran our meetings with energy and skill and set a high standard, along with many others, through the vigorous and informed criticism which he provided in response to my own line of argument. Thanks next to Michael Aho, who recruited me to undertake this rewarding project, and who, together with the Council's Director of Studies, Paul Kreisberg, made key decisions along the way about how I should proceed. My much appreciated source of unlimited practical assistance at the Council was Suzanne Hooper, who organized meetings, relayed messages, and with care and dispatch even edited my final manuscript. She was aided in preparing a summary of study group discussions by two hardworking and conscientious rapporteurs, Stephanie Hoopes and Mary Keough.

Several individual study group members deserve special thanks for the central role which they played, as commissioned paper writers or as designated discussants; they are Fred Sanderson, Ulrich Koester, Luther Tweeten, John Mellor, P.A.J. Wijnmaalen, Robert Thompson, Stefan Tangermann, and Kenneth Bader. Others provided careful critical comments directly to me at various times following our meetings, including C. Ford Runge, Julius Katz, Ed Rossmiller, Graham Avery, Don Billings, William Pearce, and Dan Pearson. Among those who took time out to offer summary reactions to the first complete draft of this manuscript were Mac Destler and Dale Hathaway, both experienced critics who have recently written books of their own on trade and agriculture, and who were thus in a position to provide a very useful form of advice. Philip Paarlberg provided an especially valuable set of detailed marginal comments and challenging criticisms. And, William Diebold intervened at key moments from start to finish with precise enquiries and with seasoned judgments which added both weight and balance to the final argument.

Beyond the confines of the Council on Foreign Relations, I owe special thanks to the National Center for Food and Agricultural Policy, at Resources for the Future, which allowed me to work on this project while simultaneously receiving their support to begin a separate but related study of international agricultural policy reform. I owe similar debts of institutional gratitude to the Center for International Affairs at Harvard University, where I have continuing access to a stimulating variety of academic and intellectual resources, and to Wellesley College, which granted me a year of sabbatical leave from my normal schedule of classroom teaching.

The advice and encouragement which I have received from my parents, Don and Eva Paarlberg, have helped more than they know. For the love and support of my wife, Marianne Perlak, I am grateful most of all.

May 1987   *Robert L. Paarlberg*

Introduction: The Need to Fix Farm Trade

Following World War II, the wealthy industrial nations of the West learned quickly that large economic efficiencies could be captured through more open international trade in manufactured products. They failed, unfortunately, to pursue comparable gains through the liberalization of agricultural trade. International agricultural trade did expand in the post-World War II period—at times, quite rapidly—but the expansion was badly marred by structural distortions and cyclical instabilities. These difficulties became increasingly troublesome to U.S. agriculture as it grew more dependent on international trade. When the international commodity trade boom of the 1970s was followed by a collapse in the 1980s, commercial and financial troubles were brought home to these vulnerable, but politically powerful, American farmers with a special vengeance. The U.S. policy response to this crisis has now threatened to touch off a bitter and damaging international agricultural trade war. In this book we shall briefly examine the sources and dimensions of the current agricultural trade crisis, and then undertake a systematic review of the policy options available for its remedy.

As recently as a decade ago, the need to fix farm trade was not at all apparent to American farmers. During the mid-1970s, world agricultural markets had entered an unusual phase of rapid expansion, and U.S. agricultural exporters found themselves on the receiving end of an unexpected international commercial windfall. World grain trade doubled during the decade, and U.S. exporters captured three-fourths of the new business.

1

The U.S. net agricultural trade surplus increased from less than $2 billion in 1971 to more than $26 billion ten years later. The share of total U.S. harvested cropland producing for export increased from 25 percent to nearly 40 percent. Anticipating that this export growth would continue, U.S. farm operators borrowed heavily to buy land and equipment at higher prices in order to expand their production capacity. Total U.S. farm indebtedness grew by roughly 60 percent.

As Figure 1 shows, this U.S. agricultural trade boom came to an abrupt end in 1981. With the onset of a world recession,

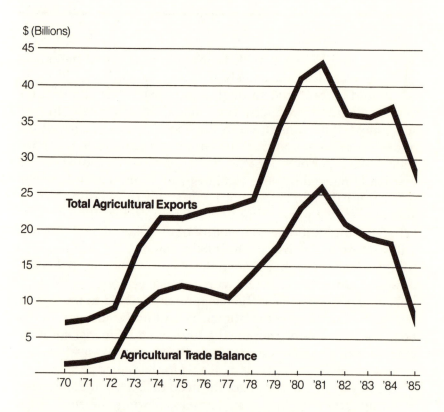

Figure 1. U.S. Agricultural Exports and Trade Balance, 1970–85
Source: Economic Report of the President 1987 (Washington: Government Printing Office, January 1987), Table B-97, p. 356.

foreign demand collapsed and U.S. exports fell. Between 1981 and 1986 the value of U.S. agricultural exports actually fell by a disastrous 40 percent, from a record $43 billion down to only $26 billion. The U.S. net agricultural trade balance, which takes imports into account, fell even more sharply, by more than 60 percent between 1981 and 1985. During one particularly distressing interlude, in the summer of 1986, the monthly U.S. farm trade balance was actually negative for the first time in more than 25 years, as the value of exports momentarily fell below imports. With this collapse of the U.S. agricultural trade balance in the 1980s, domestic commodity prices and farmland values both fell, and many U.S. farm debts became unserviceable. It became clear that the brief international commodity trade boom of the 1970s had been an insecure basis on which to rest so many farm investment and production decisions.

Given this bitter experience, U.S. agricultural producers are tempted to look for ways to make themselves less dependent upon the seemingly undependable world market. Their future prosperity requires, however, that they become more reliant on markets abroad. This is because the domestic market for agricultural products is growing too slowly, at a sluggish rate of only about 1 percent a year, reflecting both the current slow rate of population growth in the United States and the fact that the average diet is now so rich that there is little room left to expand. In contrast, domestic agricultural productivity has been growing at rates well above 1 percent, and in the near future it is forecast to grow at a rate as high as 2.4 percent.[1] If U.S. agriculture were forced to start producing only for the slow growth of the domestic market, it would have to begin quickly down-sizing itself, shedding land, labor, and capital resources at an economically inefficient and socially unacceptable rate.

Unable to prosper under the recent conditions of world farm trade, yet unable to live without trade, U.S. agriculture now faces a difficult dilemma. This book aims to provide informed guidance not only to those in the U.S. policy community who must struggle to solve this dilemma, but also to those in the U.S. food and farm sector who will have to live with the solution.

Crisis in International Agricultural Trade

The recent U.S. agricultural export collapse is only part of a much larger global farm trade crisis which has now become serious enough to capture the attention of many high-level policy-making officials who ordinarily would be paying little heed to agriculture. The world recession of the early 1980s sharply reduced global consumption of farm products, which left all exporting nations suddenly holding much larger surplus stocks. Competitive efforts to dump surpluses into shrunken world markets, by using ever larger export subsidies, proved costly and self-defeating and resulted in more downward pressure on world prices. World wheat prices fell by 45 percent between 1981 and 1987, partly in response to the lavish use of export subsidies, while the world's surplus stocks of wheat nonetheless continued to grow—increasing by almost 70 percent. World sugar prices fell by 86 percent, while surplus stocks still increased by almost half. Spending more on export subsidies in the 1980s has only added to the already high budget cost of domestic farm price support programs. U.S. farm program costs increased from less than $5 billion in the early 1980s, to roughly $26 billion by 1986. The budget cost of European Community (EC) farm subsidies and support measures roughly doubled during the same period, to reach $23 billion by 1986.[2]

Beyond the budget burdens, an even greater international risk is the growing threat to trade of a full-scale "farm trade war." American and EC agricultural trade officials have recently fallen into tense confrontations over reciprocal market access for a wide variety of food and farm products, ranging from European pasta to American citrus. This market access conflict reached a new level of intensity in 1986, when the enlargement of the EC to include Spain and Portugal sharply reduced future prospects for U.S. corn and sorghum sales. EC offers of compensation were deemed unsatisfactory, and the United States threatened to retaliate against $400 million of EC food and beverage sales. The EC responded with threats to counter-retaliate against a similar value of U.S. rice and corn gluten feed sales to the Community. These threatened retaliations and counter-retaliations were not carried out, for they were narrowly averted in January 1987 by an eleventh-hour trans-Atlantic compromise. Almost immediately, however, a new confrontation emerged over an EC proposal to impose an internal consumption tax on nondairy fats and oils, which could threaten $2.4 billion in U.S. soybean product sales to the Community. Meanwhile, competitive spending on costly and disruptive export subsidies continued to rise. This spending had already reached an absurd level in the previous summer, when the United States tried to "buy" a sale of grain to the Soviet Union, by offering an export subsidy premium of $15 a ton. The strategy failed only because the EC offered the Soviet Union an even more generous export subsidy of $125 a ton. Early in 1987, the United States bought back a part of the Soviet wheat market by increasing its subsidy offers to $44 a ton. Australian wheat exporters, caught in the crossfire, complained about being "flattened by the U.S. subsidy steamroller."

It is no wonder that these intensifying trade conflicts have now brought agriculture to the top of the international economic policy agenda. At the May 1986 Tokyo Economic Summit, the heads of government of the seven major Western industrial nations gave more discussion time to agriculture than to any other single issue, and the final declaration of that summit acknowledged for the first time the need to "adjust the structure of agricultural production in light of world demand." At the subsequent September 1986 Ministerial Meeting of the General Agreement on Tariffs and Trade (GATT) held in Punta del Este, Uruguay, an agreement was reached to give agriculture the highest priority in the next round of multilateral trade negotiations. The Ministerial Declaration that was accepted at Punta del Este launched a new round of international trade negotiations (the current so-called Uruguay Round), and emphasized the "urgent need to bring more discipline and predictability to world agricultural trade by correcting and preventing restrictions and distortions . . . so as to reduce the uncertainty, imbalances and instability in world agricultural markets."[3]

When the new trade negotiation finally got underway in 1987, even as the threats of a commodity trade war continued to escalate, the new international priority assigned to agriculture was maintained at yet another sequence of economic summit meetings. In May 1987, a Ministerial meeting of the Organization for

Economic Cooperation and Development (OECD) issued a strong statement which both endorsed the urgency of agricultural policy reform, and stressed the decisive importance of the Uruguay Round as a means to reach reform agreements. U.S. Trade Representative Clayton Yeutter described the agricultural portion of the OECD Ministerial Communiqué as "The most comprehensive statement on agricultural reform that a group of ministers has ever made." The Venice Summit in June 1987 gave endorsement to this OECD initiative, as the seven heads of government repeated their own earlier commitment to making agricultural policy adjustments "through comprehensive negotiations in the Uruguay Round." U.S. trade officials then presented the round, in July 1987, with a sweeping proposal to eliminate all farm import restrictions and export subsidies, and all internal policies that distort prices and production, within ten years time.

High-minded officials will not be able to fix farm trade through nicely worded communiqués issued at economic summits, or even through the ongoing GATT round of international trade negotiations in Geneva. Farm policies are seldom made in response to the long-run visions of high-level policy-making officials, and the game of international agricultural trade is not always played according to GATT rules. Too many of the distortions and disruptions plaguing international agricultural trade stem from the operation of costly, but nonetheless durable, domestic farm support programs. Fixing farm trade abroad will require, sooner or later, that adjustments be made in farm support programs at home. Politically, this will not be a task for the faint-hearted.

Crisis in Domestic Farm Policies

To the economist's eye, many domestic farm support programs lack justification. They produce extreme and sometimes absurd production and trade distortions. In the European Community, for example, dairy price-support policies now cost taxpayers and consumers roughly $6,200 per dairy farmer per year—and more than $400 per cow. These programs encourage dairy farmers to produce milk which is not needed within the Community at present, and which cannot be sold abroad except at a loss. Meanwhile, EC import levies make feedgrains expensive, so European dairy farmers are forced to feed their cows with products, such as citrus pulp and gluten feed, that are worth more than the milk the cows produce. In a futile effort to address this absurd situation, EC farmers recently began feeding some of their stocks of surplus butter and milk powder back to the same dairy cows that were still adding to the surplus.

The United States meanwhile struggles in its own fashion with ludicrous dairy programs that tax poor consumers, reward relatively well-to-do producers, and generate unneeded surpluses. It has been calculated that U.S. dairy programs actually cost taxpayers and consumers $26,000 per farmer, and $835 per cow.[4] In order to reduce the costly dairy surplus generated by these policies, the U.S. government in 1986 bought from dairy farmers—and slaughtered—whole herds of cattle. In the process, more than one hundred individual U.S. dairy farmers received government payments of more than $1 million. One unintended result of this buyout was lower meat prices, which angered beef cattle producers. In response to their outrage, the U.S. government decided to export live cattle and beef from the slaughtered dairy cows, which angered foreign beef exporters. The export decision indeed made little sense, for the United States is a net importer of beef.

Consumers, taxpayers, and economists may wince, but domestic agricultural "support" programs such as these have been common throughout most of the industrial world since well before World War II. The original objective of many of these programs was to ease the pain in the farm sector of having to "adjust" both to rapid productivity growth, which led to falling prices, and to urban industrial growth, which left rural incomes lagging. Farmers demanded and received price protection, which was linked to what they liked to call "parity." Too often, however, the unintended result was to make the adjustment problem even more difficult, by encouraging high-cost producers, who could be making a better living off the farm, to stay on the land and become increasingly dependent on public subsidies. Price supports also had the inadvertent effect of bidding up land prices, which meant higher production costs, and hence, few long-run gains in farm income. As the structure of farming came to depend more and more on the continuation of these subsidy programs, it unfortunately became increasingly difficult for public officials to contemplate their reform or removal. We shall see that until these highly intrusive domestic farm programs are substantially reformed at home, several varieties of farm trade failure will persist abroad.

How Has Farm Trade Failed?

The ill-effects of expensive and unreformed domestic food and farm policies are not limited to the home market. Much of agricultural trade among countries has also, as a result of these programs, become distorted and notoriously unstable. For example, between 1971 and 1973, the real export price of U.S. wheat suddenly tripled. This rapid tightening of international commodity markets, which came to be known as the "world food crisis," spawned a popular, but largely erroneous, fear that global food production and consumption trends had suddenly taken a disastrous turn. In fact, those trends had moved only slightly, but the rigidities of most national food and farm policies prevented broad-based adjustment. The result was artificial price stability inside many countries, accompanied by exaggerated price volatility in world markets. During the inflationary decade of the 1970s, the direction of that exaggerated price instability was upward, which pleased U.S. farm exporters. When inflation suddenly ended after 1981, international farm commodity prices began an equally exaggerated movement downward. This left U.S. farmers who depended on export markets out in the cold. The popular impression was that a worldwide food shortage had suddenly been replaced by a global food glut. The truth was that relatively small changes in production and consumption were again producing magnified price fluctuations in the world market because of the operation of rigid and unresponsive national policies which tended to export price instability into that market.

The distorted structure of international farm production and trade is a second feature of world agricultural markets that needs fixing. Even when world prices are relatively stable, too many farm products are being produced under subsidy in the wealthy industrial countries of the North, and not enough in the less wealthy "agricultural" countries of the South. As a consequence, too much of the world's food and farm trade is now moving, usually under costly subsidy, in the wrong direction.

In most poor nonindustrial countries, it is a politically powerful minority of urban consumers that often dictates the content of domestic food policy. These city dwellers naturally demand *low* retail food prices, set well below a market-clearing level. The predictable result is a growing internal food shortage, brought on by a rapid growth of urban food consumption unmatched by adequate rural farm production. To compensate for the shortage, governments must adopt trade policies which subsidize imports. For these nations to subsidize food imports, while their own rural land and labor resources are grossly underutilized, is distinctly inefficient and inequitable. It is like importing unemployment.

In contrast, in most wealthy industrial countries, the terms of food and farm policy are not dictated by urban consumers, but instead by a small minority of rural farm producers. These producers naturally demand *high* agricultural prices, often set well above market-clearing levels. The predictable result is a commercial surplus, caused by a combination of lagging consumption and surging production. To reduce this surplus, many industrial country governments go on to adopt trade policies which restrict imports and subsidize exports.[5]

This tendency on the part of industrial countries to adopt agricultural policies which generate an artificial surplus might seem just what is necessary to compensate for the tendency of poor countries to generate an artificial shortage. The rich can simply subsidize the sale of their agricultural surplus to the poor—and call it "food aid." In reality, this sort of international agricultural trade is an undesirable arrangement since it helps keep inefficient and inequitable food and agricultural policies in place at both ends of the relationship. Not only is this pattern of subsidized North-to-South agricultural trade demonstrably costly to consumers and taxpayers in the North, but it can also be harmful to the long-term interests of rural dwellers in the South who depend on farming for income and employment.

These North-South distortions in the structure of world agricultural trade are unfortunately matched by equally large trade distortions within the North itself. Particularly since the formation of the Common Agricultural Policy (CAP) of the European Community in the early 1960s, the location of agricultural production and the direction of farm trade in the industrial world has had less and less to do with real efficiency. High-price guarantees have allowed many less competitive EC farmers to boost yields through the lavish application of fertilizer and other expensive inputs. EC wheat farmers, for example, responded to high CAP price guarantees set at roughly twice the world level with a 19 percent increase in yield between 1972 and 1981, followed by another 27 percent increase between 1981 and 1984.[6] The resulting surplus displaced imports, and eventually had to be unloaded onto the international market through the use of increasingly expensive export-restitution payments. As a consequence between 1965 and 1983, the EC (nine nations at the time) transformed itself from a region with 20 million tons of net cereals *imports*, and a good customer for U.S. grain producers, into a region with 10 million tons of net cereals *exports*, and a menacing U.S. farm trade competitor. Relatively efficient grain producers in the United States, Canada, and Australia, who were unable to compete against lavish EC subsidies, were forced to give up valuable foreign market shares.

Policy Options for the United States

How to remedy the many problems in agricultural trade is a complex question. Chapter 1 begins with a more detailed diagnosis of the various contemporary sources of international farm trade distress. Many international farm market disruptions in recent years can be traced as much to macroeconomic circumstances as to specific malfunctions originating within the farm sector itself. Rigid national food and farm policies will be held broadly responsible, however, for worsening the effects of these macroeconomic disturbances. A comparative survey will also reveal that in recent years the food and farm policies of the EC have been, by a considerable margin, the most disruptive in this regard. It will be seen that a liberal reform of these policies would provide substantial social and commercial benefits for all nations concerned.

Chapter 2 examines current prospects for pursuing liberal agricultural policy reforms—especially within the United States and the EC—through the trading rules and negotiating procedures of GATT. Agriculture, as we shall see, has had a long and troubled history in the GATT, but in reviewing this history an effort will be made to identify the opportunities that can be seized, as well as the pitfalls that should be avoided, in the current negotiating round.

In Chapter 3, we shall consider several controversial international agricultural policy options available to the United States outside of the GATT framework. These will include, at one extreme, the cooperative "management" of international agricultural trade through formal international commodity agreements. The costs and risks associated with this approach will be seen to outweigh the probable benefits. At the other extreme, careful consideration will be given to the option of setting GATT rules aside to wage and win an aggressive farm trade "war." In the event of such a full-scale trade war, it will be shown that U.S. agricultural export interests might be the first casualty.

Chapter 4 will focus on the trade advantages that could be gained—or lost—through further modifications in U.S. domestic farm legislation. Here we shall consider the unbalanced content and the unsatisfactory performance of the recently enacted 1985 U.S. farm bill. In reviewing alternatives to current legislation, we shall point out immediately the greater difficulties that would accompany any lapse into massive unilateral U.S. farm production controls. Only a continued movement in the direction of liberal policy reform, including more realistic target price signals to farmers and the "decoupling" of program payments from production decisions, can produce a healthy long-term commercial result, both at home and abroad.

In a brief conclusion, we shall review the benefits that might come from a wise combination of policy choices in all three of these settings—inside GATT, outside GATT, and within the U.S. domestic policy arena. We shall then list a variety of essential policy initiatives outside the agricultural sector—especially in the macroeconomic policy arena—that are also necessary if the ambitious goals outlined here are to be attained.

Notes

1. *Economic Report of the President 1987* (Washington: Government Printing Office, January 1987), p. 162.
2. Geoff Miller, *The Political Economy of International Agricultural Policy Reform* (Canberra: Australian Government Publishing Service, 1986), pp. 12–13.
3. See *Economic Declaration of the Tokyo Summit*, issued May 6, 1986, and the *Ministerial Declaration on the Uruguay Round*, Punta del Este, Uruguay, September 1986.
4. Geoff Miller, *The Political Economy of International Agricultural Policy Reform, op. cit.*, p. 15.
5. For a recent summary discussion of these contrasting industrial and developing country agricultural policy tendencies, see World Bank, *World Development Report 1986* (New York: Oxford University Press, 1986), Chapters 4–6. For an earlier and more quantitative comparative assessment, see Malcolm D. Bale and Ernst Lutz, "Price Distortions in Agriculture and Their Effects: An International Comparison," *American Journal of Agricultural Economics*, vol. 63, no. 1 (February 1981), pp. 8–22.
6. Kenneth L. Robinson, "The Consequences of U.S. and European Support Policies," in Randall B. Purcell, ed., *Confrontation or Negotiation: United States Policy and European Agriculture*, Reports From a Public Policy Study of the Curry Foundation (New York: Associated Faculty Press, 1985), p. 128.

One

Agricultural Trade in Disarray: Sources and Dimensions of the Problem

Not all agricultural trade difficulties stem from misguided farm policies. Much of the recent cyclical instability in international farm trade has its origins, instead, in unbalanced and undisciplined fiscal and monetary policies, especially those of the United States, which have badly destabilized the larger macroeconomic environment in which farm trade must function. In this chapter we shall first attempt to distinguish between the *nonfarm sector* and the strictly *farm sector* sources of agricultural trade problems. We shall then judge the dimensions and the consequences of the latter in greater detail.

The Macroeconomics

It would be a serious error to attribute all of the boom and bust in world farm markets in recent years to flawed farm trade policies. Much of the cyclical disruption has been caused, instead, by extreme fluctuations in worldwide income growth rates and currency exchange rates. The volatility in the macroeconomic environment can be, in turn, ascribed largely to a lack of balance and discipline in fiscal and monetary policies. Efforts to fix farm trade which do not address these nonfarm policy sources of disruption will be doomed to frustration.

Rapidly changing macroeconomic circumstances put a heavy strain on farmers, especially when a sudden boom is followed by a sudden bust. This is because most of the capital stock employed in modern agriculture cannot be easily or quickly transferred to alternative applications. Idle land and farm machinery are costly to own, and the accelerated movement of labor out of farming can involve uniquely painful adjustments in lifestyle and personal identity. Modern agriculture is a capital-intensive and trade-sensitive industry, highly vulnerable to external macroeconomic disruptions. In an earlier day, when the agricultural sector was still largely self-sufficient, farmers could afford to spend most of their time worrying about low commodity prices, or the weather. Today, because farmers must borrow so heavily to purchase expensive equipment and inputs, and because so many of their goods have become tradable internationally, they must also worry about fluctuating interest rates, inflation rates, and currency exchange rates.

Unfortunately for U.S. agriculture, boom and bust global macroeconomic instability has been a fact of life since 1971 when the "Bretton Woods" system of fixed international currency exchange rates finally collapsed. World commodity markets—including farm markets—have borne much of the burden of this collapse. The Bretton Woods system had been designed under U.S. leadership to impose enough discipline on the fiscal and monetary policies of individual countries to keep currency values in rough alignment. A cumulative loss of U.S. fiscal and monetary policy discipline in the 1960s, combined with the emergence of sizable and largely unregulated international capital markets, put the system under stress. The United States finally lost it ability to manage this system in 1971, and the general obligation to maintain fixed exchange rates was soon discarded. By 1973 a flexible or "bloc-floating" exchange rate system, which was essentially free of any formal national macroeconomic policy obligations, had emerged by default. It was the United States which abused this new freedom the most by holding in place, for most of the rest of the decade, the same highly inflationary fiscal and monetary policies which had done so much to undermine the Bretton Woods system in the first place.

The first global macroeconomic consequence of these developments was an interlude of rapid worldwide growth in the early 1970s, accompanied and undermined by increasing rates of global inflation. Annual real GNP growth rates among the industrial countries rose from 3.6 percent in 1971 to 5.5 percent in 1972, and up to 6.3 percent by 1973. Among the developing countries (LDCs), growth rates increased even more rapidly, up to 6.2 percent in 1972 and 7.4 percent in 1973. The attendant surge in demand for everything from oil to metals to agricultural products was reflected in an across-the-board commodities price boom. This boom was to some extent sustained, later in the decade, by the undisciplined lending of windfall commodity profits—particularly "petrodollars" from the Organization of Petroleum Exporting Countries (OPEC)—into the eager hands of consumption-driven borrowers in industrial and developing countries alike. With inflation raging and plenty of money to borrow, real interest rates fell so low that nations were tempted to stop saving and move even more deeply into debt. Holdings of existing wealth moved out of interest-bearing securities and into the consumption and stockpiling of goods, pushing farm commodity prices still higher. The inefficient organization of world farm markets added still more to this sudden run up in world farm prices, as we shall see. Nevertheless, it was a larger macroeconomic environment of highly inflationary growth that got the process started.

For U.S. agricultural exporters, this macroeconomic environment was fun while it lasted. The same U.S. macroeconomic policies that had done so much to trigger inflationary growth worldwide were also driving down the exchange rate of the dollar, ensuring that U.S. farm commodities would be competitively priced abroad. While global farm trade was expanding fourfold during the 1970s, U.S. agricultural exports were actually increasing sixfold. The U.S. share of total world agricultural trade increased as a consequence, from 14.4 percent in 1971 to a record 19.3 percent by 1981.[1]

The cumulative result was that the total value of U.S. farm exports suddenly tripled between 1971 and 1974, and then nearly doubled again by the end of the decade. U.S. farm operators, often encouraged by the policies of their own government, drew the erroneous conclusion that the surging world farm market demands of the 1970s were a durable consequence of some fundamental change in the world's food supply and demand situation. Instead, they were just a temporary consequence of rapid income growth in a highly inflationary global macroeconomic environment which, unfortunately, proved to be anything but durable.

By the end of the 1970s, rapid income growth—even with more inflation—had become too difficult to sustain, even with more borrowed money. The growing inflation (now dubbed "stagflation") was becoming socially intolerable, particularly after the second major oil price shock of 1979. It was at this juncture that U.S. macroeconomic policy underwent a sudden and profound change. New leadership came to the Federal Reserve Board, determined to tighten the U.S. money supply as much as necessary to bring inflation under control. Since U.S. fiscal policy remained essentially undisciplined, this tightening had to be excessively severe. The result, by 1981, was much higher real interest rates and the onset of a sharp worldwide recession.

The impact of the recession was felt only briefly in the United States, thanks to the huge "supply-side" tax cuts of 1981 which provided a short-run stimulus to U.S. consumption. Yet these tax cuts required so much foreign borrowing to finance the resulting federal budget deficit that within five years the United States was transformed from a net creditor into the world's single largest net debtor nation.

In part because of these much heavier U.S. claims on foreign capital, the impact of the 1981–82 recession proved more lasting abroad. Total foreign real GDP growth rates, which had averaged a strong 5.5 percent in 1970–74, and which maintained at a respectable 3.7 percent between 1975 and 1979, fell to a low of 1.6 percent in 1981, and then averaged only 2.4 percent between 1982 and 1986. Since 1981, growth has effectively come to a halt within some of the more heavily indebted developing countries. Real GDP growth in Latin America, for example, fell from a strong 6.3 percent yearly average during the 1970s, to a *negative 0.8 percent* average between 1981 and 1983.[2]

Accompanying these lower foreign economic growth rates were decreases in foreign food consumption levels. Foreign grain consumption, which had increased at an average rate of 34 million tons per year throughout the 1970s, fell to only an average 19-million-ton yearly increase during the first half of the 1980s. Worldwide, the growth in per capita food consumption slowed in the 1980s to less than two-thirds the pace of the 1970s.[3] Inefficiencies in the world's farm trading system meant that this sudden drop in global food consumption demand would lead to a disproportionate collapse in international farm commodity prices.

On the downside of this macroeconomic boom and bust cycle, U.S. farm exporters were doubly punished. The same sudden tightening of U.S. monetary policies which helped trigger the recession also drove up dollar exchange rates—by roughly 70 percent between 1980 and 1985—obliging U.S. exporters to fight for their share of the smaller world market under an enormous price disadvantage. Having used low dollar exchange rates to capture a disproportionate share of the market expansion in the 1970s, U.S. farm exporters now had to absorb a disproportionate share of the pain as markets contracted in the 1980s. The U.S. share of world agricultural exports fell from 19.3 percent in 1981 down to only 16.6 percent by 1985. As a consequence, the absolute value of all U.S. agricultural exports fell even more sharply from $43 billion in 1981 all the way down to just $29 billion in 1985, and still lower to just $26 billion in 1986.

If so much of the recent boom and bust in U.S. and world agricultural exports can be traced to unstable macroeconomic conditions, then how can we hope to fix farm trade without prior progress on global macroeconomic reform? Here we shall not deny the importance of improved macroeconomic policy management, without which the future of all global economic growth remains at risk. If growth continues to falter, there will be little that even the wisest agricultural trade policies can do to improve export prospects for U.S. agriculture. It has been estimated that every one-half percentage point change in world economic growth translates into roughly an 8.6 percent increase (or decrease) in world demand for meat, and as much as a 10-million-ton (15 percent) change in foreign demand for U.S. grain. By similar magnitudes, slumping world economic growth can mean an unavoidable U.S. farm export decline.[4] Nor can we look with any great comfort upon prospects for macroeconomic reform in the near future. The 1983–86 U.S. economic "recovery," which may now have finally run its course, was fueled all along by a nonsustainable pattern of heavy foreign and domestic borrowing. With the resulting U.S. foreign and domestic indebtedness now reducing the room for fiscal and monetary policy maneuver in Washington, an unprecedented burden of macroeconomic policy leadership will have to fall into the hands of reluctant and relatively unpracticed officials in Japan and Germany. There can be no firm guarantee of their success.

The obvious importance of improved macroeconomic management is a point to which we shall return in our final chapter. Having recognized its significance here, we must now turn to an equally powerful set of "microeconomic" variables which operate more narrowly within the food and farm policy sector. These variables may not be the most profound cause of cyclical disruption in world farm markets, but they nonetheless aggravate the disruptions. Moreover, when seeking an explanation for the large structural distortions found in today's world farm markets, we shall find that these narrowly defined food and farm policy variables have been decisive.

The Microeconomics: Domestic Food and Farm Policies

Narrowly defined food and farm policies contribute to farm trade malfunctions in at least two separate ways. First, they tend to aggravate short-run fluctuations in world farm prices. Second, they tend to create long-run distortions in the location of world farm production and consumption, and therefore in the direction and volume of world farm trade.

Destabilized World Prices

Farm commodity prices fluctuate by nature, if only in response to sudden changes in production caused by unpredictable weather. A price change under these circumstances is a healthy signal to undertake appropriate production and consumption adjustments. Unfortunately, many nations try to spare their citizens the inconvenience of making such adjustments. In order to do so, they administer policies (such as "variable levies") which prevent their own internal food and farm prices from fluctuating. When cyclical shortages or surpluses develop, citizens in these nations have no incentive to adjust because prices remain constant. These countries end up by making most of the necessary adjustments to their new internal supply situation through changes in the volume of their international trade at the border. By making adjustments at the border through trade, rather than internally through changes in their own domestic production and consumption, these nations are in effect forcing their own burden of adjustment onto producers and consumers abroad. They are "exporting instability" into the world's agricultural marketplace.

Nations which use this technique to stabilize internal prices will usually have to pay a substantial cost in terms of lost foreign exchange. This is because they make their foreign trade adjustments with a blind eye toward international price trends, buying if necessary from a rising world market, or selling if necessary into a world market gone slack. If these nations are wealthy enough, they may consider this an acceptable price to pay for the internal food and farm price stability they are after.

Obviously, there is an upper limit to the number of nations that can simultaneously adopt such an inward-looking price stabilization strategy. The cyclical adjustment burden which one nation chooses not to bear can be exported, but not eliminated; sooner or later it must be borne by producers or consumers somewhere. There are two types of trade-dependent countries that usually get caught absorbing the burdens. First are some of the developing countries, especially those lacking the foreign exchange resources necessary to "buy" domestic price stability through constant trade adjustments. Second are those few wealthy industrial countries—such as Australia, Canada, and the United States—which are traditionally farm product exporters, and which are willing to accept some price instability at home in return for the ability to capture commercial farm trade advantages abroad. Unfortunately, since most other large agricultural trading nations—including Japan, the EC, and the Soviet Union—do not leave their borders open to world price fluctuations in this fashion, a large burden of the price instability tends to fall on those few that do.

This burden of price instability can be measured by comparing the observed "coefficient of variation" in today's world farm prices to the smaller coefficient of variation that would be experienced if one or more nations were to liberalize their food and agricultural policies, allowing international price signals to cross their borders.[5] Using this technique in a study of world wheat markets, Maurice Schiff has estimated that the variability of world wheat prices could be reduced by 48 percent if all countries were to end their illiberal wheat policies.[6] Two other analysts, Rodney Tyers and Kym Anderson, have used a more ambitious computer model which simulates the effects of policy liberalization in more than six different commodity markets. They have calculated that industrial country liberalization alone could go a long way toward reducing the international price variability of most major temperate-zone commodities—wheat by 33 percent, coarse grains by 10 percent, rice by 19 percent, sugar by 15 percent, and dairy products by as much as 56 percent.[7]

Among the Western industrial countries, which ones have been responsible for the worst international price destabilizing effects? In the world's all-important wheat and coarse grain markets, this dubious distinction has fallen most often upon the EC. Using data from the late 1970s, Tyers and Anderson have estimated that if the EC alone liberalized its agricultural policies, coefficients of price variation would fall almost as far (93 percent for wheat, and 100 percent for coarse grains) as if all the industrial market economies—including the United States, Canada, and Japan—were to liberalize together.[8]

EC cereals policies are highly destabilizing because of the variable inport tax—the so-called "variable levy"—which the Community applies to most farm products at its border.[9] This levy, which is designed to keep efficiently produced foreign products out of the high-priced Community market, is "variable" in the sense that it is recalculated daily in order to equal the difference between the low international price and the much higher EC threshold price. When international prices drop, the levy automatically increases to compensate. When international prices rise, the levy automatically declines.

It is in this fashion that world price signals are prevented from entering the EC. If there is a momentary international shortage of cereals, and if prices rise globally, EC consumers and producers do not receive the appropriate signal to produce more and consume less. That burden is shifted to others.[10] Conversely, if there is a momentary surplus in world cereals markets, EC producers will receive no automatic signal to reduce production, the surplus will be aggravated, and producers outside the Community will suffer.

Now that the EC has emerged in the 1980s as a significant net exporter of cereals, it must use "variable export restitutions" as well as variable import levies to maintain internal price stability. Export restitutions are cash subsidies paid to EC exporters in order to make high-priced EC cereals disposable at the lower world market price. Whenever the international price falls, EC export-restitution payments per bushel must increase to meet the competition. When world prices fall sharply, this can become an expensive proposition for the Community budget, especially when high internal production incentives are simultaneously pushing up the volume of surplus commodities that must be disposed of in this fashion. The only short-run alternative, and hardly an inexpensive one, is to allow a buildup of carryover stocks.

There should be a more obvious remedy to the problem of coping with unstable world farm market prices. If price destabilizers, such as the EC, joined together to multilaterally reduce all the variable border taxes and border subsidies which jam international price signals today, world prices would immediately become more stable—as the previous estimates by Schiff and Tyers and Anderson would indicate. Furthermore, the high cyclical adjustment costs associated with letting price signals cross the border could be reduced for everyone. When all parties adjust simultaneously, the burden on each becomes lighter and less onerous. A multilateral liberalization of national food and agricultural policies would reduce price instability in world markets to such an extent that the costs of remaining open to those markets would become tolerable for all.[11]

Distorted Trade Structures

Not only do nations adopt food and farm policies which destabilize the *condition* of world farm markets; they also embrace programs which distort the long-term *structure* of production and trade. In some instances these programs encourage relatively high-cost farmers to produce too much, while in other cases they encourage relatively low-cost farmers to produce too little. The trade patterns that grow out of these distorted structures of production fall far short of an efficient ideal.

The most extreme structural distortions can be traced to high domestic commodity price guarantees which many Western industrial democracies offer to their farm producers. These have a universal tendency to stimulate wasteful surplus production and to stifle internal consumption when passed on to domestic consumers. These high-price-guarantee policies, in combination with the *low* food and farm price guarantees maintained by many poor countries, cause too much of the world's production to be located in the rich industrial world of the North, rather than in the supposedly "agricultural" world of the South. More specifically within the North, too much agricultural production is currently located in the EC and Japan, to the relative disadvantage of the more efficient farmers in Canada, Australia, and the United States.

The precise magnitude of these structural distortions remains a matter for debate. The only means of measurement is to create, as a basis for comparison, mathematical models of imaginary alternative world markets entirely free of government interference, and where agricultural commodity prices would be allowed to rise or fall as much as necessary to balance supply with demand. The models which have been created for this purpose have numerous drawbacks and differences, but all are at least in rough agreement on the structural changes that could be brought about by various forms of trade liberalization.[12]

Beginning with agricultural trade relations between rich and poor countries, there is general agreement that trade liberalization by the rich would produce significant farm trade gains for the poor. Alberto Valdes and Joachim Zietz have compared the total value of LDC farm imports and exports under real world conditions (during 1975–77) to the values that would have been seen, assuming a simulated 50 percent reduction in the protectionist tariffs on ninety-nine agricultural commodities that are imposed by the rich member-nations of the OECD. According to their rough calculations, such a liberalization by OECD members could have increased the agricultural export revenues of all LDCs by roughly $6 billion—or about 11 percent—in 1977. These trade gains would be realized mostly through increased sales to the OECD countries of sugar, beverages, tobacco, meats, coffee, and vegetable oils. It is true that OECD liberalization would also lead to slightly higher international prices for some of the temperate-zone crops—such as cereals—that are imported by many LDCs. But the resulting increase in LDC farm import costs would be less than one-fourth as large as the increase in export revenues, according to Valdes and Zietz, leaving LDCs on balance much better off.[13]

The generally higher food import prices that most LDCs would encounter under an OECD liberalization scenario would not only be more than offset by higher farm export earnings. If passed along (in a liberal fashion) to local food producers, they would also help to stimulate local farm production and rural income growth within poor countries, thereby lifting what is usually a large internal constraint to balanced agricultural and industrial development. Too many LDCs today hinder their own internal growth prospects by passing artificially low international food prices on to their own rural producers.

Among industrial countries, the gains from agricultural liberalization would differ considerably depending on current levels of farm sector protection. In those nations where farm sectors are most heavily protected, such as Japan and the EC, the overall social gains from liberalization would be large due to more efficient resource use and gains from trade, but the farm sector gains would be negative. In those countries where farm sectors are less heavily protected, such as Australia, Canada and the United States, overall social gains would be smaller, but farm sector losses would be smaller as well. In some commodity markets, efficient farmers in these nations could even profit from liberalization.

One particularly ambitious mathematical simulation of the effects of full agricultural trade liberalization on industrial countries has been produced at the International Institute for Applied Systems Analysis (IIASA) in Laxenburg, Austria. It compares the simulated effects of OECD agricultural trade liberalization to a "reference scenario" which assumes no change in current policies. The study concludes that an OECD farm trade liberalization could increase the volume of international trade in some farm products substantially, boost most international farm prices, and redirect trade to the relative advantage of agricultural producers and exporters in Canada, Australia, and the United States, as well as throughout most of the developing world. Relative farm sector losses would be suffered primarily in the EC and in Japan.[14]

Under this full liberalization scenario, trade volume would increase by the year 2000 (compared to the reference scenario) most rapidly for rice (37 percent) and for animal products (12–35 percent). World market prices of agricultural products, relative to nonagricultural products, might increase overall, on a trade-weighted basis, by 9 percent. Export price increases for cereals, protein feed, and animal products specifically would be higher by a 10–20 percent range, and for dairy products by as much as 30 percent. Agricultural producers in Canada, Australia, and the United States would enjoy increases in "agricultural GDP" of 17 percent, 3 percent, and 2 percent, respectively, as a result of a general liberalization. In the EC and Japan, however, agricultural GDP would decline, by 7 percent and 5 percent, respectively. Agricultural acreage would expand in Canada, Australia, and the United States, but decrease once again in the EC and Japan.[15]

Product by product, the distribution of producer gains and losses from free trade would show greater divergence. Both the EC and Japan would reduce their highly protected grain production (including rice) substantially, as well as their meat and dairy output. Canada and Australia might increase their meat and dairy production, in the process using more of their own grains domestically to feed livestock, and the United States would increase its specialization in producing and exporting grains. The volume of U.S. wheat exports in the year 2000 might be increased 19 percent through liberalization (compared to the reference scenario), and U.S. exports of coarse grains by 12 percent.

However, the United States would also become a substantial importer of both sugar and dairy products.[16]

There is a general concurrence between the results of the IIASA exercise and estimates published by the World Bank, from a parallel liberalization study prepared by Rodney Tyers and Kym Anderson.[17] This study estimates the international price and trade effects of liberalization by first measuring the "nominal protection coefficients" of a variety of mostly temperate-zone crops, in thirty countries (or groups of countries) using 1980–82 data. Some of these measurements of protection, by country and by commodity, are reproduced in Table 1.

A nominal protection coefficient is simply the price of a commodity within a nation, divided by the (higher or lower) price at the border. Where agriculture is protected by national policy,

Table 1
Nominal Protection Coefficients for Producer Prices of Selected Commodities in Industrial Countries, 1980–82

Country or Region	Wheat	Coarse Grains	Rice	Beef & Lamb	Pork & Poultry	Dairy Products	Sugar	Weighted-Average[a]
Australia	1.04	1.00	1.15	1.00	1.00	1.30	1.00	1.04
Canada	1.15	1.00	1.00	1.00	1.10	1.95	1.30	1.17
EC[b]	1.25	1.40	1.40	1.90	1.25	1.75	1.50	1.54
Other Europe[c]	1.70	1.45	1.00	2.10	1.35	2.40	1.80	1.84
Japan	3.80	4.30	3.30	4.00	1.50	2.90	3.00	2.44
New Zealand	1.00	1.00	1.00	1.00	1.00	1.00	1.00	1.00
United States	1.15	1.00	1.30	1.00	1.00	2.00	1.40	1.16
Weighted-average	1.19	1.11	2.49	1.47	1.17	1.88	1.49	1.40

[a]Averages are weighted by the values of production and consumption at border prices.
[b]Excludes Greece, Portugal, and Spain.
[c]Austria, Finland, Norway, Sweden, Switzerland.

Source: World Bank, *World Development Report 1986* (New York: Oxford University Press, 1986), Table 6.1, pp. 112–13.

the resulting coefficient will be above 1.00. The higher the coefficient, the higher the level of nominal protection. The Tyers and Anderson estimates of the comparative levels of farm trade protection, when read with care, can tell us a great deal about existing distortions in the structure of world farm production and trade. They also provide clues as to why some countries are more protectionist than others.

Note from Table 1 that protection coefficients vary considerably within the industrial world. The highest levels of protection, by a significant margin, are found in Japan. Australia, Canada, and New Zealand are generally the least protectionist. The EC is markedly more protectionist than the United States, but considerably less protectionist than Japan. The EC is even less protectionist than "other Europe."

Does this mean that the two largest OECD sources of international agricultural trade distortion are Japan and non-EC Europe? Definitely not. The different levels of protection must be adjusted by the various capacities of domestic producers—and consumers—to *respond* to that protection. In nations such as Japan, or Sweden, where agricultural resources—such as flat and fertile land—are scarce, an extremely high coefficient of protection for wheat and coarse grains does not generate much additional production. In many EC countries, however, agriculture production resources are more abundant. In some parts of France and Britain, for example, the structure of farming is highly efficient. Where this is the case, even a modest level of protection can be enough to distort trade badly by generating a large volume of surplus production.

When the CAP was first created in Europe, negotiations over common commodity price levels did not take these production response capabilities adequately into account. Unfortunately, the price levels initially established for dairy and cereals were set near the top of the existing pre-CAP member-country range. The high prices traditionally received by relatively inefficient and nonresponsive German dairy farmers were suddenly generalized to relatively efficient dairy farmers in countries such as Holland, and as a result production went out of control. The same phenomenon occurred to a lesser extent in cereals, where relatively high German prices (reduced by only a nominal 10–15 percent) became the standard throughout the Community, suddenly giving much stronger production incentives to more efficient and responsive cereals producers elsewhere, especially in the French Paris Basin. Britain's entry into the Community in 1973 contributed still more to unconstrained cereals production when the relatively efficient grain producers of East Anglia also gained access to higher CAP prices.

Prior to Britain's entry into the EC, its grain yields had been increasing at only a moderate rate—up from 3.1 tons per hectare in 1960 to only 4.5 tons in 1977. Then, responding to the more lavish use of inputs like fertilizer rendered affordable by higher CAP prices (which became fully available to Britain's producers in 1978), yields began increasing rapidly to reach 5.4 tons per hectare by 1982, and 6.6 tons by 1984. If British yields and net trade in grains had followed the pre-CAP trend, that country would still be a net importer today, of 6 or 7 million tons of grain. Given access to CAP protection, however, Britain has emerged as a net exporter of 3 or 4 million tons of grain.[18]

The EC, which in the mid-1960s was importing 20 million tons of grain, is now—largely as a consequence of the CAP—*exporting* roughly 15 million tons. This is equivalent to a 35-million-ton reduction, over this period, in the size of the world grain market available to more efficient producers elsewhere. If subsidized EC grain production is not brought under control, some Community officials have calculated that an exportable surplus as large as 80 million tons might be available by the early 1990s.[19]

The commodity-by-commodity patterns of protection indicated in Table 1 also deserve comment. It is no accident that the coefficient of protection maintained by the United States for sugar is considerably higher than for wheat or coarse grains. Since it is an importer of sugar, the United States can afford to grant a high level of protection to domestic producers simply by placing quotas on cheap foreign imports. Import quota restrictions are costly not only for excluded foreign producers, but also for U.S. domestic sugar consumers because they drive up internal "market" prices. They have, however, the unbeatable political advantage of costing taxpayers nothing. If an equivalent level of protection for U.S. sugar growers had to be provided at the taxpayer's expense, through visible budget outlays rather than through an invisible tax on consumers, U.S. sugar support programs would probably have to be scaled back.

Note that in markets where the United States is a large net *exporter*, such as wheat and coarse grains, agricultural protection levels are much lower. This is because in export-oriented product markets the cost to society of offering protection cannot so easily be hidden at home, or passed on to foreigners. The only way to protect U.S. cereals exporters against foreign competition is to use such things as cash export subsidies, which are vulnerable to political attack both by budget officials and by those who rightly oppose the use of the taxpayer's money to transfer large visible benefits to foreign consumers.

As a general rule, the inclination to protect is stronger when agricultural sectors are import-competing, and weaker when they are export-competing. Canada and Australia, which have farm sectors even more export-oriented than in the United States, are the least protectionist. Japan, which has a farm sector deeply penetrated by imports, is not surprisingly the most protectionist. Japan's overall food self-sufficiency level, which is relatively low at just 73 percent, is actually continuing to *decline*. Japan is self-sufficient in rice, but in grain and soybeans its self-sufficiency levels are a mere 33 percent and 5 percent, respectively.[20] The fact that self-sufficiency continues to decline in Japan despite high levels of agricultural protection is one more reason to look elsewhere for the most serious contemporary sources of agricultural trade distortion.

In sharp contrast to Japan, the EC remains extremely protectionist even though its food self-sufficiency is high rather than low, and rising rather than falling. Historical comparisons are complicated by the changing membership of the EC, but despite the entry of Britain (which was a large net *importer* when it joined the Community in 1973) self-sufficiency ratios in the EC have been going up sharply, as Table 2 indicates. By 1983, in contrast to earlier times, the EC-9 had become more than 100 percent self-sufficient in wheat, sugar, cheese, beef and veal, pigmeat, and poultry. In each of these product markets, despite rising

Table 2
Degree of Self-Sufficiency of European Community
(percent)

	1962 (EC-6)	1973 (EC-9)	1983 (EC-9)
Wheat	100	104	125
Maize	NA	56	72
Sugar	97	91	144
Cheese	98	102	108
Butter	101	101	123
Beef and veal	87	91	104
Pigmeat	99	101	101
Poultry	98	103	110
Fruit	86	79	81
Vegetables	112	94	97

Source: D. Gale Johnson, Kenzo Hemmi, Pierre Lardinois, *Agricultural Policy and Trade*, A Report to the Trilateral Commission: 29 (New York: New York University Press, 1985), Table EC-4, p. 109.

self-sufficiency, the EC continues to maintain relatively high nominal protection coefficients.

The relatively high protection coefficients originally established within the EC in the mid-1960s must have seemed affordable to taxpayers at the time (they were always costly to consumers), because the Community was still a net importing region. High protection even meant higher budget revenues, gained through import levy collections. Unfortunately, the responsiveness of EC producers to high CAP prices has now transformed the Community into a net exporting region. Protection from more efficient foreign competitors must now increasingly be provided through expensive cash outlays for export restitutions. It may be hoped that these rapidly increasing CAP budget costs, associated with the Community's new export-dependent posture, will eventually force some reduction in the level of producer protection guarantees.

Are There Gains from Liberalization?

Using the estimates of nominal protection presented in Table 1, plus a model of world agricultural markets built around supply-and-demand equations for thirty countries or country groups and seven different commodity groups, Tyers and Anderson have presented their own detailed estimates of the percentage changes in international prices and trade volume that might accompany a multilateral food and farm policy liberalization by all OECD countries. Even more interesting, they have also presented estimates of the changes that would be noticed if only the EC, or only Japan, or only the United States were to liberalize. The estimates, presented in Table 3, substantiate the general conclusions of the IIASA study mentioned earlier. More specifically, they confirm the suspicion that substantial benefits to efficient international farm trade can only be captured if adequate liberalization measures are embraced by the EC.

Note from Table 3 that Tyers and Anderson estimate the international price and trade volume effects of OECD liberalization to be rather small, at least from the assumed 1980–82 starting point. World prices would firm up a bit (because surplus production would no longer be dumped onto the global market through export subsidies), and trade volume would expand slightly in most cases (because import restrictions would be lifted all around). The total magnitude of these effects, however, would be quite modest, particularly in wheat and sugar markets. The total volume of wheat trade might even decline a bit. Changes in the *location of production* and the *direction of trade* would be more dramatic. Within the EC, production of feed grains, beef, dairy products, and sugar would all decline, and imports would rise. Japan would go from self-sufficiency in rice to roughly a 50 percent dependence on imports, and its self-sufficiency in beef would decline from 66 percent to 8 percent. In the United States, exports of feed grains would increase—by an estimated 18.4 million tons—and imports of dairy products and sugar would increase substantially. With higher world prices, the United States would turn from a net importer to a net exporter of beef.[21]

What deserves special attention in Table 3 is the estimated impact, specifically in coarse grains markets, of *unilateral* agricultural trade liberalization by the United States. If the United

Table 3
**International Price and Trade Effects of Liberalization
of Selected Commodity Markets, 1985**

Country or country group in which liberalization takes place	Wheat	Coarse Grains	Rice	Beef & Lamb	Pork & Poultry	Dairy Products	Sugar
			Percentage change in international price level following liberalization				
EC	1	3	1	10	2	12	3
Japan	0	0	4	4	1	3	1
United States	1	-3	0	0	-1	5	1
OECD	2	1	5	16	2	27	5
Developing countries	7	3	-12	0	-4	36	3
All market economies	9	4	-8	16	-2	67	8
			Percentage change in world trade volume following liberalization				
EC	0	4	0	107	3	34	-5
Japan	0	3	30	57	-8	28	1
United States	0	14	-2	14	7	50	3
OECD	-1	19	32	195	18	95	2
Developing countries	7	12	75	68	260	330	60
All market economies	6	30	97	235	295	190	60

Note: Data are based on the removal of the rates of protection in effect in 1980–82. Data for the EC exclude Greece, Portugal, and Spain.

Source: World Bank, *World Development Report 1986* (New York: Oxford University Press, 1986), Table 6.7, p. 129.

States had liberalized its agricultural policies unilaterally in 1985, note that international coarse grains prices would not have been firmed up—they would have actually *fallen* by 3 percent. This is because domestic grains policy at that time (still under the provisions of the 1981 farm bill) was biased toward unilateral reductions in cropland, which were designed to reduce farm program costs in the short run by firming up domestic commodity prices. Higher U.S. commodity prices, however, were then transmitted, through American exports, into the world marketplace, where less efficient foreign competitors saw them as a marvelous opportunity to expand production, undersell U.S. exporters, and capture larger market shares at the expense of the United States. While domestic production was being cut to prop up prices, foreign production and foreign exports expanded. As will be argued in Chapter 4, if the United States can break the bad habit of unilaterally firming up world prices for less efficient foreign competitors, if necessary by unilaterally liberalizing some if its own agricultural policies, then those competitors will be left with less leeway to keep their own illiberal policies in place.

The implication of these analyses seems clear. If national food and agricultural policies were liberalized, world agricultural prices would become more stable, the total volume of trade would grow, and both the structure of global agricultural production and the direction of trade would become more efficient. This would provide large net welfare gains to practically all nations concerned. In fact, Tyers and Anderson have attempted a rough calculation of the welfare gains that would accompany a full liberalization in those seven commodity markets which they examined. Their model predicts that all the industrial market economies together would gain $46 billion from liberalization, and the developing countries $18 billion. Interestingly enough, the only big net losers would be the Soviet and East European nonmarket economies, which would lose the access which they now enjoy, through depressed and distorted world farm markets, to artificially cheap supplies of food.[22]

The Liberalization Dilemma

If the potential gains from agricultural trade liberalization are so large and so widespread, then why have the Western industrial nations yet to find a way to liberalize? Resistance comes, quite naturally, from minority groups—especially farm producer groups—which have grown comfortable with the explicit protection they enjoy under current arrangements. According to yet another Tyers and Anderson scenario, if all the OECD nations were to liberalize their agricultural policies simultaneously, consumers and taxpayers could expect a large *net gain* of $104 billion, but farm producers might have to sustain a *net loss* of $56 billion. It is the resistance of self-interested and well-organized farm producer groups that most often halts progress toward farm trade liberalization.

Can agricultural trade liberalization still be a good idea if so many farm interest groups are against it? The apparent unity among farmers on this question is deceptive. Relatively efficient farmers, including most of those in the United States that are currently producing for export, would stand to lose little from liberalization and gain much. For the American farmer, liberalization would mean fewer heavily subsidized competitors abroad, and fewer political barriers in the path of their exports. The only big losers in the U.S. agricultural sector would be the highly inefficient and inflexible producers (and processors) of products such as sugar and dairy, who have in many instances *grown* inefficient and inflexible over the years precisely because of their government protection from foreign competition. Under liberalization, the interests of this vulnerable minority would have to be protected, ideally through direct payments issued independent of production or trade. At any rate, protectionist dairy and sugar programs should not be permitted to stand in the path of liberalization initiatives that could benefit U.S. agriculture as a whole.

It is an error to believe that the health of U.S. agriculture—or for that matter European agriculture—depends upon establishing and maintaining high levels of agricultural "protection." Over the long run, it depends on just the opposite—on access to a competitive environment in which the efficient use of resources is consistently rewarded. The dubious long-run value of protection is to some extent confirmed by comparing the welfare of U.S. farmers working in product markets where heavy protection has long been granted, to the welfare of farmers working in product markets where protection is essentially absent. For instance, U.S. dairy farmers receive near total protection at the border from cheap imports, as well as lavish internal price guarantees, but, in general, they have had just as many income problems as the essentially unprotected American producers of hogs, cattle, poultry, and most fruits and vegetables. Likewise, modestly protected U.S. wheat growers are usually in greater difficulty than relatively unprotected soybean growers. In addition, the "protection" received by sugar growers, in the form of import quotas and high-price guarantees, has in some ways made things worse for cane and beet producers. This is because high domestic sweetener prices have helped bring into production, since the 1970s, a competing non-sugar sweetener—high fructose corn syrup (HFCS). By 1984, U.S. domestic consumption of this competing corn-based sweetener had actually surpassed the domestic consumption of sugar.

Policies of agricultural protection frequently succeed in boosting farm commodity prices, but higher farm prices are a poor guarantee of long-run agricultural sector prosperity. This is because 85 percent of all U.S. agricultural economic activity now takes place off the farm, either upstream or downstream from the shrinking number of individuals in the modern food production chain that are still farming.[23] Many downstream agricultural workers (plus livestock producers) are purchasers of farm commodities, and are actually damaged by high commodity prices. Even on farms themselves, high commodity prices are quickly lost to rising land prices and rents, once farmers begin bidding against each other to gain the means to produce more of what they now can sell at the higher price. The result, beyond the very short run, can be a continuing decline in what producers end up seeing as "farm income." Even highly protected farmers in the EC have experienced this disappointing effect. Despite generous farm price supports, average real farm income in most EC countries under the CAP has not been raised significantly relative to nonfarm income.[24]

Instead of trying to "protect" farmers by fixing prices or by otherwise intervening in commodity markets, governments would accomplish more by subsidizing farm income with direct cash payments. Such payments do more for farm income than trade distorting commodity programs. For the United States, as an example, it has been estimated that government commodity programs which distorted markets and cost taxpayers $20.2 billion in 1986, managed to add only $12.5 billion to farm income. The rest of what was spent either went to off-farm interests, or was lost entirely. As much as 40 percent of the value of all U.S. government expenditures on farm export subsidies goes straight to *foreign* consumers.[25] By replacing such wasteful trade interventions with direct cash payments to farmers, the United States could simultaneously boost farm income and reduce the farm budget burden on taxpayers.

Equity questions cannot be avoided in any discussion of protectionist farm policies. In the United States, where median family income is only $27,735, government payments to commercial farms in 1986 (farms with annual sales above $100,000) averaged $42,000 per farm. The social justification for transferring wealth in this direction is, to say the least, not clear. Nor are these large commodity program payments to farms equitably distributed. Table 4 shows the distribution of program disbursements by farm sales class. Note that a small number of giant-sized farms (the 2.1 percent which enjoy annual gross sales of $500,000 and up) receive 14.7 percent of all government program outlays, with an average of above $100,000 per recipient. This is three times the average granted to "family farm" recipients in the mid-sized $100,000–$250,000 sales class range. Sometimes the recipients of these U.S. farm support payments are ludicrously undeserving of the benefit being conveyed. In 1986, one large California cotton producer received more than $12 million in payments. The Crown Prince of Liechtenstein, as a partner on a Texas rice farm, received a subsidy from U.S. taxpayers of more than $2 million.[26] At the other extreme, nearly one-half of all U.S. farms currently under the greatest "financial stress," with both high debts and a negative cash flow, receive no government payments at all, because they do not happen to be producing "program" commodities.[27]

Protectionist farm policies which operate through the marketplace by pushing up prices, automatically give the greatest benefits to the larger farmers who produce most of what is sold. As Table 4 indicates, nearly one-third of all crop and livestock sales in the United States are made by just 2.1 percent of all

Table 4

Distribution of U.S. Government Commodity Program Outlays by Sales Class[1]

	Percent of all farms	Percent of total crop & livestock sales	Percent of total outlays	Percent of farms receiving outlays	Average outlay per recipient
Sales Class					
$500,000 and up	2.1	31.3	14.7	56	$105,000
$250,000–$499,999	5.1	20.0	22.0	62	$ 58,000
$100,000–$249,999	14.6	26.7	38.1	66	$ 33,000
$40,000–$99,999	18.4	14.3	19.8	57	$ 15,000
Less than $40,000	59.8	7.7	5.4	18	$ 4,000

[1]Data from *1985 Farm Costs and Returns Survey*. Outlays include direct government commodity program payments and net CCC loans.

Source: USDA, *Farmline*, vol. 8, no. 1 (December–January 1987), p. 5.

farms. Furthermore, even if commodity program benefits were more carefully targeted by farm size, equity problems would continue to arise between generations. Since benefits are so quickly capitalized into higher land values, the older and better established farmers who own their own land will continue to gain in relation to younger farmers trying to buy land to get a start.

It is not surprising, given all these equity concerns, that the heavy use of protectionist farm programs, in both Europe and the United States, has been accompanied by a continued "loss" of small and mid-sized farms and an increasing preponderance of much larger giant-sized farms. These largest farms are not necessarily the most efficient, but access to excessive farm program benefits gives them—in the current policy environment—a useful economy of scale. The fact that program benefits remain essentially untargeted, despite the implied disadvantage for efficient and socially desirable "family farms," is often testimony to the political power, within the organized farm community, of larger farm operators.

For political and social reasons, it is both necessary and desirable that governments provide income support to farmers. Fortunately, there are better ways to provide this support than through agricultural "protection." Instead of trying to provide benefits to farmers through restraints on trade, or through other crude and untargeted forms of commodity price manipulation, governments should see the value of providing cash payments directly to deserving farm producers. Direct cash payments can be targeted on a more equitable basis, and can be "decoupled" from commodity prices, thus giving producers the freedom to plant in response to real market demands. Decoupling the delivery of farm income support from farm production decisions in this fashion would allow all concerned to capture the efficiency gains from liberalization that were described earlier. These efficiency gains would, in turn, make the cost of providing direct and well-targeted farm income support that much more affordable.

The objective of this book—to fix farm trade—should not be pursued against the interests of farmers. Fortunately, the liberalization of farm trade that we advocate here is precisely in the interest of most U.S. farmers, whether all of their traditional political spokesmen realize it or not. Responsible U.S. policymakers who seriously want to "protect" farmers should think twice before moving further in the direction of price-boosting restrictions on production and trade. The increasing closure of world markets to U.S. farmers that would accompany these restrictions would only force the agricultural sector to shrink more rapidly. Policymakers would be better advised to search for ways to remove existing restrictions, at home and abroad, to the anticipated advantage of most U.S. farm trade. Those policymakers would also be well-advised, as we stressed at the outset, to do a better job of managing the volatile macroeconomic environment in which U.S. agricultural trade must now function.

If liberalization is the objective, then what are the most promising tactical means to reach that goal? Agricultural policy has both a domestic and an international dimension; therefore the pursuit of liberalization requires policy initiatives both at home and abroad. Since not all international behavior can be governed by rules, the pursuit of more liberal international agricultural trade relations must take place both inside and outside of GATT. In the chapters that follow, we shall examine in systematic fashion the appropriate steps toward liberalization that might be taken by U.S. agricultural policymakers in these three separate settings—within the GATT, in negotiations and trade relations with other nations outside of GATT, and in the domestic agricultural policy arena at home.

Notes

1. "Studies Prepared for the Use of the Republican Members of the Joint Economic Committee, Congress of the United States, by the Congressional Research Service, Library of Congress." Joint Economic Committee, Joint Committee Print, 99th Cong., 2d Sess., October 1, 1986, Table 1, p. 50.
2. U.S. Department of Agriculture, Economic Research Service, *Agricultural Outlook*, (November 1986), Table 3, p. 36.
3. "Global Trends in Agricultural Supply and Demand," Remarks by Robert L. Thompson, Assistant Secretary for Economics, U.S. Department of Agriculture, at Outlook '87, the 63rd Annual Agricultural Outlook Conference, U.S. Department of Agriculture, Washington, December 2, 1986.
4. Fred H. Sanderson, "An Assessment of Global Demand for U.S. Agricultural Products to the Year 2000," *American Journal of Agricultural Economics*, vol. 66, no. 5 (December 1984), p. 584.
5. A coefficient of variation is the expected deviation from the long-term average price in any particular year as a percentage of the average price.
6. Maurice W. Schiff, "An Econometric Analysis of the World Wheat Market and Simulation of Alternative Policies, 1960–80," ERS Staff Report AGES850827 (Washington: U.S. Department of Agriculture, International Economics Division, 1985).
7. World Bank, *World Development Report 1986* (New York: Oxford University Press, 1986), Table 6.9, p. 131.

8. Kym Anderson and Rodney Tyers, "European Community Grain and Meat Policies: Effects on International Prices, Trade and Welfare," *European Review of Agricultural Economics*, vol. 11, no. 4 (1984), pp. 366–94, Table 2, reproduced in Kym Anderson and Yujiro Hayami, *Political Economy of Agricultural Protection: The Experience of East Asia* (Sydney: Allen and Unwin, 1986), Table 5.2.

9. Variable levies are also applied to Community imports of rice, olive oil, sugar, milk, and milk products.

10. For a brief time in 1974, in fact, when world cereals prices went so high as to exceed the EC threshold price, this variable import levy system was automatically transformed into a variable *export tax*, effectively preventing EC cereals supplies from being used abroad to ease the shortage in international markets.

11. EC officials would even discover, to their pleasure, that a very small amount of increased price variability within the Community might give *private* agricultural producers and traders an incentive, which they do not currently have, to carry larger buffer stocks. With the private sector playing this useful role, the burden imposed on taxpayers by Europe's persistent quest for internal price stability could be further reduced.

12. The results of such models must always be used with caution. For a summary comparison of recent modelling efforts, see Rachel N. Sarko, "Agricultural Trade Model Comparison: A Look at Agricultural Markets in the Year 2000 With and Without Trade Liberalization" (Discussion Paper RR87-01, National Center for Food and Agricultural Policy, Washington, November 1986).

13. Alberto Valdes and Joachim Zietz, "Agricultural Protection in OECD Countries: Its Costs to Less Developed Countries" (Research Report 21, International Food Policy Research Institute, Washington, 1980).

14. IIASA Food and Agriculture Project, *Towards Free Trade in Agriculture* (Laxenburg: International Institute for Applied Systems Analysis, 1986), Table 5.4.

15. Ibid., Figure 5.3, Table 5.1, and Table 5.4.

16. Ibid., Table 5.11.

17. World Bank, *World Development Report 1986, op. cit.*, Chapter 6.

18. U.S. Department of Agriculture, Foreign Agriculture Circular, Grains, FG-3-86 (March 1986), p. 8.

19. Graham J. Avery, "The Future of Cereals Policy in the EC," European Weed Research Society, Proceedings of Stuttgart Symposium, 1986, p. 32.

20. D. Gale Johnson, Kenzo Hemmi, and Pierre Lardinois, *Agricultural Policy and Trade*, A Report to the Trilateral Commission: 29 (New York: New York University Press, 1985), p. 114.

21. Results from the Tyers and Anderson model probably overstate the gains that the U.S. farm sector would enjoy from OECD liberalization. This is because the model excludes oilseeds, and U.S. soybean exporters currently profit from CAP restrictions on cereals imports.

22. World Bank, *World Development Report 1986, op. cit.*, p. 131.

23. Robbin S. Johnson, "Implications for U.S. Agribusiness Strategies," Statement presented at Outlook '87, the 63rd Agricultural Outlook Conference, U.S. Department of Agriculture, Washington, December 12, 1986.

24. I.R. Bowler, *Agriculture Under the Common Agricultural Policy* (Manchester: Manchester University Press, 1985), p. 204.

25. Ulrich Koester and Ernst-August Nuppenau, "The Income Efficiency of Government Expenditure on Agriculture Policy," *Intereconomics*, (March/April 1987), pp. 74–75.

26. *Economic Report of the President 1987, op. cit.*, p. 157.

27. "Who Gets Those Farm Program Payments," *Farmline*, vol. 8, no. 1 (December-January 1987), p. 3.

Two

How to Fix Farm Trade: Inside GATT

I f liberalizing international farm trade is our objective, one of the most obvious settings in which to pursue that goal becomes the General Agreement on Tariffs and Trade (GATT). GATT is the world's only institution with a record of success in promoting nondiscriminatory trade liberalization, and a new round of GATT negotiations has now been launched with agricultural trade issues squarely on the agenda. In this chapter we shall take a careful look at what GATT is likely to deliver in the current Uruguay Round—based in part on what GATT has and has not been able to achieve in the past. We shall then review a range of alternative GATT negotiating strategies for the United States. It will be necessary, in the end, to warn against relying exclusively on GATT negotiations to fix all that is wrong with international farm trade. The key to successful use of GATT, as we shall see in the chapters to follow, rests with a variety of supporting measures that must be taken outside of its formal framework.

Why the GATT?

There is a great attraction, at least in theory, to pursuing agricultural trade liberalization primarily through a multilateral institution such as GATT. Economic logic tells us that for those farmers that will be losing their protection, the "pain" associated with liberalization will be reduced *if all nations liberalize at the same time.* If a nation were to liberalize unilaterally, its society as a whole would benefit; but its agricultural sector could face a larger burden of adjustment by suddenly having to compete "unprotected" against foreign trade rivals who still enjoy state subsidies. If all nations liberalize at the same time, then all societies will profit without any one country's agricultural sector having to face an oversized adjustment burden. If all agricultural sectors are losing subsidy protection simultaneously, the sense of unilateral disadvantage is avoided, the actual size of the adjustment imposed on each can be reduced, and larger social welfare gains can be realized, making the necessary compensation of disadvantaged farm interests that much more affordable.

Efforts have been made to estimate the size of the adjustment cost reductions that could be gained through strategies of *multilateral* liberalization. The IIASA computer model used to simulate the effects of a multilateral farm trade liberalization (described in Chapter 1) has also been used to simulate the smaller social gains and the larger farm sector losses that might accompany various "unilateral" liberalization initiatives. According to this model, a U.S. decision to liberalize its farm trade unilaterally would succeed in increasing domestic economic growth overall (compared to a reference scenario of no policy change), but growth within the farm sector itself would not increase, and might even fall slightly (by one-half a percentage point by the year 2000).[1] In contrast, if all OECD nations were to liberalize simultaneously, U.S. GDP would increase at an even faster rate, and U.S. farm sector GDP would go up as well, by 1.8 percent compared to a reference scenario of no policy change. U.S. farm price parity might decline slightly under multilateral liberalization, but only by about 2 percent (as opposed to more than 6 percent under unilateral liberalization), leaving U.S. farm income essentially "unaffected," given a higher volume of production and trade.[2] From the vantage point of the U.S. farm sector as a whole, according to these estimates, multilateral liberalization should have an unbeatable political attraction over unilateral liberalization.

The advantage of using multilateral institutions to pursue liberalization has been endorsed by knowledgeable advocates of farm trade reform both inside and outside the U.S. government.

A recent study by the Trilateral Commission concluded that "Although there are good economic arguments for greater market orientation even with other countries standing still, the chances of significantly reducing the degree of protection provided agriculture are far better with all trilateral areas (Europe, Japan and North America) moving together. The fear that lowering protection unilaterally would result in a flood of imports with little or no prospect of offsetting advantages in international markets makes greater market orientation most unlikely unless carried out in concert with other major importers and exporters of farm products."[3] Taking up this theme, U.S. Trade Representative Clayton Yeutter has described agricultural liberalization as a global problem requiring a "global solution."[4] The U.S. Undersecretary of Agriculture has been even more blunt in endorsing multilateralism: "The bottom line is that we must reject the 'go it alone' approach and move to a global solution. The new round of trade negotiations is a major opportunity for making that move. . . . [T]he international bargaining table is where the solution lies . . ."[5]

For those who believe in the "global" approach to agricultural trade liberalization, the current Uruguay Round of GATT negotiations in Geneva provides the most obvious venue for pursuing a multilateral agreement. Launched at Punta del Este in September 1986, this latest round of multilateral GATT negotiations is pledged—according to its own Ministerial Declaration—to "bring more discipline and predictability to world agricultural trade by correcting and preventing restrictions and distortions, including those related to structural surpluses, so as to reduce the uncertainty, imbalances and instability in world agricultural markets."[6] With top-level support and endorsement from a variety of other multilateral institutions—including both the OECD and the yearly Western Economic Summit process—these GATT negotiations are now at the center of attention for those who hope for international farm policy reform.

Origins, Rules and Procedures

The General Agreement on Tariffs and Trade is an evolving international contract, subscribed to by ninety-two governments, consisting of specific reciprocal trade obligations, general trade rules, and dispute-settlement procedures. The original General Agreement, concluded in 1947, was intended to be just one part of a larger postwar International Trade Organization (ITO). The ambitious and controversial ITO Charter was never submitted to the suspicious U.S. Congress for ratification, because of fears that Congress would never agree to giving up its own powers in this area. But GATT somehow survived, and proceeded to take on a useful life of its own.

The fundamental trade principle of GATT is nondiscrimination—expressed in the form of a requirement that all countries must be treated as well as the "most favored nation." The principal objective of GATT, under postwar U.S. leadership, became "liberalization"—the reduction (in a nondiscriminatory fashion) of existing barriers to trade. Governments can use GATT negotiating rounds to seek mutually advantageous bargains, based on concessions and compensations offered in a reciprocal manner. They can, however, resist becoming a party to any bargain which they find unattractive. The quasi-legal rules and procedures of GATT, which are written into its Articles, have all been authored at one time or another by the sovereign national governments involved. The GATT Secretariat has never been a strong source of independent international authority over trade.

This distinct GATT approach has enjoyed spectacular success since 1947 in securing multilateral reductions of customs tariffs on manufactured trade. Seven successive rounds of GATT negotiations have reduced average tariffs on manufactured trade from their original postwar level above 40 percent all the way down to a level of less than 5 percent today. During this period of successful operation, GATT membership increased fourfold, and several dozen other "nonmember" nations agreed to apply GATT rules to their trade as well. Now even the Soviet Union has begun seeking an affiliation with GATT. Despite the deference paid to national sovereignty, GATT rules and procedures are not taken lightly when trade disputes arise. The U.S. International Trade Commission (ITC) has judged GATT dispute-settlement procedures to be "adequate" for managing all but the "most contentious" disputes.[7]

GATT would seem to be, in every respect, the best available instrument for pursuing multilateral agricultural trade liberalization. The fact remains, however, that previous efforts to use GATT to liberalize farm trade have failed badly.

GATT Rules on Agriculture

Those hoping to use GATT to liberalize agricultural trade should be aware of the difficulties they will face. GATT's ability to open up agricultural trade was undermined from the start when certain explicit allowances for *illiberal* agricultural trade practices were written into its rules, including the use of quantitative import restrictions and export subsidies. The United States was the champion of this effort to obtain separate treatment for agriculture in GATT, and America's trade rivals have never let the United States forget it. Vigorous attempts by the United States to tighten these original rules in subsequent rounds of multilateral GATT negotiations have for the most part failed. In addition, agricultural issues have not fared well under the dispute-settlement procedures of GATT. These procedures, which have been judged adequate in other trade areas, have repeatedly been unable to resolve highly contentious disputes over agriculture.

It was originally at the insistence of the United States that Article XI of GATT (entitled "General Elimination of Quantitative Restrictions") was written to contain an important exception for "agricultural or fisheries" products. Quantitative import restrictions were to be explicitly permitted for such products, provided that restraints were also placed on domestic production. If the United States had been unsuccessful in obtaining this allowance in Article XI, some important existing U.S. domestic farm support programs would not have been able to function, and Congress would have rejected U.S. participation in GATT from the start.

This originally feeble standard on quantitative import restrictions was to be weakened even further, once again at the insistence of the United States. In 1951 a GATT finding was reached that the United States had "infringed" on Article XI by imposing quantitative restrictions on dairy imports, while failing to apply the requisite restraints on domestic production. Congress, however, rejected the implications of this finding by amending basic farm legislation in Section 22 with a requirement that the administration impose quantitative restrictions, or special fees, whenever domestic support programs were endangered by free trade.[8] The enactment of this legislative provision made it necessary for the United States in 1955 to ask for, and to receive, a permanent "waiver" from the provisions of Article XI. The United States has since then used this waiver to go forward at various times with dairy, beef, and sugar import restrictions which have been unaccompanied by production restraints, and which therefore do not measure up even to the more lenient GATT rules that the United States itself had originally helped to write.

The existence of the waiver for the United States has naturally weakened the ability of GATT to apply a strict interpretation of Article XI to the trade behavior of others. According to recent testimony by Deputy U.S. Trade Representative Alan Woods, "Countries do not feel compelled to live closely by the GATT obligations on quantitative restrictions when the United States is exempt from them by virtue of the waiver."[9] In part because of the waiver, it has been more difficult for the United States to complain effectively in GATT about the quantitative import restrictions, variable import levies, and monopoly state-trading practices that so many other nations use at times to close their borders to agricultural imports.

GATT rules for agriculture were also written with an exception that permits the use of export subsidies. Article XVI of the GATT begins by prohibiting both direct and indirect export subsidies, even including instruments such as "deficiency payments" which can distort trade indirectly by encouraging output expansion. The Article goes on, however, to make yet another exception for agriculture and for other "primary products." The only restriction imposed on agricultural export subsidies is an ambiguous stipulation that they not be used to capture a "more than equitable" share of world trade, taking into account an undefined "previous representative period."

U.S. domestic agricultural interests once again helped to secure this permissive rule, and when this general "derogation" allowing farm export subsidies was re-examined by GATT in 1958, it was the United States that took the lead in its defense. Later in the 1960s, U.S. traders began to realize that the allowance for farm export subsidies could more easily be exploited by free-spending foreign competitors such as the EC, but by then it was too late to reimpose discipline.

If the rules of GATT, as originally written, have sanctioned too many illiberal farm trade practices, then why not use the current Uruguay Round of trade negotiations to tighten the rules? The history of past GATT negotiating rounds is instructive, and somewhat discouraging, on this score.

Disappointments in Past Rounds

With the benefit of hindsight, the 1961–62 Dillon Round of GATT negotiations was an opportunity to tighten agricultural trade rules *before* the final creation, in 1962, of the highly protectionist European Common Agricultural Policy (CAP). This opportunity was for the most part lost. During the Dillon Round, negotiators were preoccupied with reducing the common external tariff for manufactured products created by the EC, so they left most agricultural issues to the side in a series of "standstill" agreements. At the end of the round, the United States declared its intent to negotiate "at a later date" the GATT status of EC variable import levies, which were then coming into effect. This variable levy system, protectionist as it was, had been carefully crafted with existing GATT rules in mind, and would therefore prove difficult for American negotiators to challenge.

During the Dillon Round, U.S. negotiators were required to operate under trade legislation which allowed them to discuss at most a 20 percent tariff reduction, and which forced them to conduct the negotiations on a laborious item-by-item basis.[10] Still, it was by proceeding on this basis that U.S. negotiators managed by the end of the round to secure what remains today the single largest trade concession ever granted to the United States in GATT—a "zero-duty binding" on EC imports of oilseeds (such as soybeans), oilseed meals, and some other nongrain feed items such as corn gluten feed. Neither the United States nor the EC realized how large this concession would later loom when higher grain prices in Europe would begin to increase the commercial attraction of these substitute imported feed sources.

The 1963–67 Kennedy Round was the first explicitly announced test of the power of American trade negotiators to liberalize agricultural trade in GATT. By the time these negotiations began the threat posed by the CAP to U.S. agriculture was abundantly clear. U.S. negotiators therefore entered the negotiations demanding that any further reductions in U.S. customs tariffs on manufactured goods be firmly linked to a liberalization of EC variable import levies for agriculture. President Lyndon Johnson promised domestic farmers that "The United States will enter into no ultimate agreement unless progress is registered toward trade liberalization on the products of our farms as well as our factories."[11] U.S. farm exporters still remember with some bitterness that this promise was not kept. The linkage between manufacturing and agriculture proved impossible to maintain since it faced so much resistance that it threatened the entire negotiation; thus EC variable levies remained in place.

For the first several years of the Kennedy Round, EC negotiators in Geneva did not even have the authority to discuss agricultural trade concessions with their American counterparts, because at the time CAP policymaking was paralyzed by a major crisis in Brussels over internal voting procedures. The dispute was finally resolved in 1966—after France actually withdrew from the EC Council of Ministers for six months—through an agreement to apply a "unanimity" rule to all major EC policy decisions on agriculture. Unfortunately, this rule gave nations such as France an effective veto over any concessions on variable levies that EC negotiators might otherwise have considered making to the United States in Geneva.

The EC was also unable to negotiate seriously about lowering farm trade barriers during the Kennedy Round because it was at that very moment moving toward much higher common farm price levels at home. Between 1959 and 1968, as the EC's common farm price system was gradually going into full effect, cereals protection levels within the Community increased dramatically, from 14 percent up to 72 percent, according to one U.S. estimate.[12] All that the EC could propose in Geneva was a multilateral freeze on levels of agricultural support, to take place *after* this increase in common EC prices in Brussels had been completed. Such a freeze in "margins of support" (*montant de soutien*) would have placed the EC, with its common producer prices at roughly twice the world level, on a legal par in GATT with more liberal trading nations such as Australia, where producer prices for all agricultural exports were essentially at the world level. Since this freeze in margins of support was to have been maintained against an artificially *fixed* international reference price, it would also have legitimized the EC's uniquely disruptive use of *variable* import levies. The EC was in effect trying to secure, through GATT, international legitimacy for its own increasingly illiberal agricultural trade policies.

The failure of the Kennedy Round to produce significant agricultural trade liberalization must also be blamed on the United States, which was no better prepared than the EC to consider meaningful changes in its domestic farm programs. It would be unrealistic to ask for agricultural trade concessions from the EC without offering something in return, but the only thing that may have interested the Community—a liberalization of U.S. dairy programs—could not have been credibly put forward by American negotiators, because it would have immediately required changes in U.S. domestic farm legislation, an exclusive prerogative of the U.S. Congress.

Congress had been willing to delegate unprecedented across-the-board tariff-cutting authority to U.S. negotiators prior to the Kennedy Round, in the Trade Expansion Act of 1962. Most agricultural trade restrictions, however, are *nontariff* barriers (NTBs)—such as import quotas—which result from separately authorized domestic farm legislation. How to negotiate changes in such congressionally controlled domestic farm programs presented a political problem, and indeed a Constitutional problem, that was never squarely addressed by the U.S. negotiators during the round. The relevant congressional authorities were never even approached. Legally, it might have been possible for U.S. negotiators to end-run congressional restrictions by offering limited agricultural concessions to the EC strictly on the basis of some of the "discretionary" farm program powers then available to the Secretary of Agriculture. But to use such a short-cut tactic against the will of agricultural committees in the Congress would have meant a certain political disaster for liberal agricultural trade policy in the long run.[13]

Some limited progress on agricultural reform was made in the Kennedy Round, but only in the restricted area of customs tariff reductions. The United States made agricultural tariff concessions covering $610 million of farm imports, in return for concessions from others covering $870 million of imports. The negotiations on EC variable levies, and on other nontariff agricultural trade barriers, however, proved fruitless.

GATT enthusiasts sometimes argue that international trade negotiations can be a helpful deterrent to protection even when they do not produce an agreement. Simply talking about prospective multilateral bargains in Geneva can be enough to discourage protectionist domestic farm lobbies from taking illiberal policy initiatives at home. Recall, however, that internal EC farm policies during the Kennedy Round became steadily more protectionist. Moreover, soon after the negotiations began, the U.S. Congress passed legislation restricting meat imports; Britain (not yet an EC member) offered higher incentives to livestock producers; and the United States increased internal milk price guarantees.

Liberal-minded U.S. trade officials vowed to do a better job on agriculture during the 1973–78 Tokyo Round of GATT negotiations. They began early, by making a more serious effort to secure in advance the negotiating authority necessary to trade U.S. concessions on nontariff barriers in exchange for changes in EC farm programs. Specifically, U.S. negotiators wanted the ability to put protectionist U.S. dairy and livestock programs on the table in return for EC concessions on grains. The U.S. Department of Agriculture (USDA) calculated that such a trade-off might boost total American agricultural exports by as much as $10 billion, while imposing only about a $1 billion import increase on the adversely affected parts of the U.S. farm sector.[14] Unfortunately, the USDA calculation was leaked to the domestic farm community, and the favorable political reaction that should have come from export-oriented grain producers was drowned out completely by angry objections from import-competing dairy and livestock groups, who understandably felt threatened.

As a consequence, when the administration went to Congress in search of nontariff barrier negotiating authority for the Tokyo Round, it encountered strong resistance. The office of the U.S. Trade Representative (then called the Special Trade Representative) wanted authority to offer NTB concessions to trade partners, subject only to a congressional "veto" within a specified period of time. But a wide range of U.S. farm interest groups, led by milk producers, successfully pressured the Senate Finance Committee into adjusting the 1974 Trade Act to require a more difficult vote of *positive approval* from Congress on NTB agreements.[15] In the end, a "fast track" procedure was adopted, to make sure these congressional votes would at least be taken on a timely basis (within 90 days), and also with a clean "up or down" vote (no amendments permitted).[16] Even when placed on this fast track, however, the anticipated need to win positive congressional approval for NTB agreements helped to undermine the administration's bold negotiating strategy for agriculture.[17]

Even beyond agriculture, the negotiators in the Tokyo Round found it difficult to make much progress on NTB reductions. Despite considerable efforts, negotiators failed to agree on a code for the most commonly used nontariff method of evading GATT rules on manufactured trade—the use of "voluntary export restraints." A variety of other widespread NTBs to nonfarm trade were left uncontrolled as well: including industrial targeting, state-owned monopolies, misaligned exchange rates, subsidies through tax concessions, performance requirements governing foreign investment, licensing in services, antitrust regulations, and violations of international property rights.[18]

Overall, the Tokyo Round produced only two significant achievements for U.S. agriculture. First, Japan did agree to tariff concessions on $1.2 billion U.S. agricultural exports, including the binding of its zero duty on soybeans. This was to be implemented gradually over an eight-year period, and it now has been. An agreement was also reached to pursue a relaxation of Japan's many quota restrictions on imported farm products, including beef and citrus. This agreement expired in 1984, with U.S. farm exporters still less than satisfied with the final result. Subsequent efforts to reduce Japanese import quotas have been no more than marginally successful, and have been made through bilateral channels to a large extent outside of GATT.

A second achievement for U.S. agriculture in the Tokyo Round was the negotiation of a new Subsidy Code, intended to tighten the permissive language originally found in Article XVI on the use of "primary" product export subsidies. The Code still permitted these export subsidies, provided that the subsidizer not obtain more than an equitable share of world trade or materially undercut the prices of other suppliers to the same market. The definition of "more than equitable share" was expanded under the Code to include displacement of other exporters in third-country markets. Furthermore, the "previous representative period" for determining such shares was defined more precisely as the "three most recent calendar years in which normal market conditions existed." The new Code also created an elaborate multilateral mechanism for the settlement of disputes which enabled signatories to enforce their rights under this Code.[19]

The first significant test of the dispute-settlement mechanism in the new Subsidy Code was a disappointing failure from the U.S. vantage point. It was the case of EC wheat flour export subsidies. In February 1983, after six years of delay, the Subsidies Code mechanism yielded only an ambiguous non-verdict: it could not deny that EC subsidies had probably caused "undue disturbance to normal U.S. commercial interests," but it could not be proved that they caused price undercutting, or that the EC gained a "more than equitable" share of the market. A GATT panel of experts acknowledged that the EC wheat flour export share had increased considerably, which would not have been possible without export subsidies. They also recognized that the subsidies may have reduced sales opportunities for the United States. Yet they refused to go so far as to conclude that the EC had used its subsidies to gain a more than equitable market share, on the grounds that the terms of the Subsidy Code were not sufficiently "operational, stringent, and effective."[20] It was at this point that the United States initiated direct retaliation against the EC with a disruptive wheat flour export subsidy program of its own.

The United States has not had much more success in its many other attempts to resolve farm export subsidy disputes through GATT. One GATT panel did decide in favor of an American protest against subsidized EC pasta exports, which were penetrating the U.S. domestic market directly, but the EC blocked the panel decision by arguing that pasta export subsidies should be permitted to offset the high cost of durum wheat inside the Community. The EC also ignored a panel recommendation that it alleviate injury to the United States by reducing its preferential treatment of citrus imports from Mediterranean countries. Finally losing patience on these two issues, the United States responded in November 1985 with a unilateral 25–40 percent increase in its own tariffs on imported pasta. The EC then counter-retaliated by increasing customs duties on fresh lemons and walnuts, and by raising pasta subsidies even further. This escalating dispute was in the end contained, at least temporarily, through direct bilateral discussions between the United States and the EC, but again outside of GATT.[21]

GATT rules did assist the United States to some extent in its efforts to force the EC to provide compensation for the U.S. farm trade losses suffered in Spain and Portugal following the enlargement of the Community in 1986. The United States argued that it was entitled, under Article XXIV, to an "intraline" credit, meaning that compensation for farm trade damages resulting from the expansion of a free trade area would have to come in the form of offsetting *agricultural* trade concessions. EC officials had originally hoped that the United States would accept improved industrial trade access to Spain and Portugal as adequate compensation. The United States used the ensuing 1986–87 compensation negotiations, which were required under GATT, as a useful setting in which to press its case. The EC eventually agreed to some limited compensations in the agricultural sector, including a promise to import 2.3 million tons (over a four-year period) of non-EC corn and sorghum into Spain under reduced levies. This sort of bilateral quota arrangement was not entirely in keeping with liberal GATT principles.[21] But an illiberal compensation for the U.S. trade loss was perhaps better than no compensation at all.

Explaining GATT's Weak Performance in Agriculture

There are several reasons for GATT's relatively weak past performance in agriculture. First in a purely technical sense, GATT is not well-suited for negotiations on obstacles to international trade in agriculture, because they are mostly *nontariff* barriers. As such, they are not as uniform, as transparent, as measurable, nor as unchanging in their effects on trade as simple customs tariffs. On analytic grounds alone, this makes reaching negotiated GATT agreements more difficult.

Nontariff agricultural trade barriers also present a problem for GATT because they are directly linked to the operation of separately authorized domestic farm programs. Illiberal border measures are usually necessary to help these market-distorting domestic programs to function. The border measures cannot be eliminated until the domestic programs have been changed, but the trade officials who negotiate border measures are usually without authority to offer significant concessions on domestic farm program reforms.

This lack of negotiating authority is as much a problem for the EC as it is for the United States. Only the full Agricultural Council of Ministers in Brussels can authorize significant changes in EC farm policy. Reform of EC farm policy can be difficult enough even without having to consider "concessions" to foreign trade rivals. Since individual member countries, by citing a vital national interest, can veto any significant Community-wide agricultural policy actions taken by the Council, these decisions must necessarily be laboriously prepared and painstakingly balanced to preserve consensus. Such finely balanced Council decisions are often taken as "package deals," so they cannot easily be disaggregated at a later date and subjected to piecemeal change—least of all in the context of an international negotiation.

The "Eurocrats" from the Commission who are sent to negotiate for the Community in GATT are not given adequate authority to work toward agreements that might imply substantial changes in the existing mechanisms of the CAP. EC negotiators in Geneva do their best to disguise this lack of authority by resorting to a variety of delaying tactics, by pointing out the frequent inconsistencies in the negotiating demands of others, and by placing on the table contentious issues which they know their counterparts do not have authority to discuss. The ensuing deadlock may look like a "failure," but it is usually just what protectionist farm interests inside the EC are after.

Protectionist farm interests in the United States will also look for ways to bring GATT negotiations to a stalemate, and then to profit from the deadlock. While deadlocked talks are underway, they can demand more subsidies for themselves as "bargaining chips" in the negotiation or as "tactical" instruments to force concessions from their adversaries. If the talks then fail to produce these concessions, U.S. farm groups can demand still more protection as an appropriate retaliation against "intransigent" foreign competitors. Such efforts on the part of domestic U.S. farm interests to manipulate the conduct of trade negotiations to their own illiberal advantage have already begun in the current round.[23]

There is also a deeper explanation for the relatively poor performance of GATT in agriculture. An international deal on agriculture in GATT is difficult to achieve because heavily protected farm producers, especially in the EC and Japan, would suffer large relative losses from such a deal, while lightly protected farm producers elsewhere would reap sizable relative gains. With a multilateral farm trade liberalization, consumers and taxpayers in the EC and Japan could expect to gain, but most agricultural producers would face difficult adjustments. Even if made somewhat easier by a simultaneous agricultural liberalization in the more lightly protected OECD countries, the anticipated losses would be enough to set a majority of EC and Japanese farm interests squarely against the sort of GATT liberalization agreement that Australia, Canada, and the United States are looking for.

By one estimate, even if all OECD nations liberalized at the same time, the ratio of agricultural prices to nonagricultural prices inside the EC might still fall by 9 percent, almost as large as the 12 percent drop that might be experienced if the EC farm sector were to liberalize alone. So the relative gain to EC farmers from entering a multilateral agreement to "share the adjustment cost" of liberalization is quite small. This is due to the fact that much of the adjustment, in either case, would have to be made by EC farmers themselves. By the same token, U.S. farmers favor multilateral over unilateral liberalization not because it is an equitable way to proceed, but precisely because it would imply larger relative adjustments for more heavily protected farmers outside the United States.[24]

Because U.S. and EC farm sector interests in liberal reform are so poorly matched, the familiar GATT requirement that a "balance of concessions" be maintained is hard to satisfy. A pattern emerges in which the United States is forever making liberalization demands, and the EC is forever saying no. The demands and the refusals take on infinite variation, but progress toward liberal reform is consistently blocked.

Prospects for the Uruguay Round

Can we be confident that the current Uruguay Round will produce a break in the pattern of stalemate on agricultural issues in GATT negotiations? This time around, there are both reasons for greater optimism, and new grounds for concern.

On the positive side, narrowly based farm sector interests may find it more difficult today to undermine the current round of negotiations, because increasing farm program budget costs throughout the OECD have made nonagricultural policy officials more interested than ever in a favorable outcome. This is not only true in the United States. The EC budget expenditures, two-thirds of which go to agriculture, are now running almost $5 billion above revenues, and they may soon require yet another politically difficult increase in member-country value-added tax (VAT) contributions. The interests of EC finance ministers and taxpayers, which were largely absent from the negotiating table in previous rounds, will today provide a healthy new impetus for reform.

In addition, unlike in previous multilateral negotiations, the United States will not be the only demandeur. Prior to the Punta del Este Ministerial meeting which launched the round, a group of fourteen "non-subsidizing" countries led by Australia, the so-called Cairns Group[25], added its voice to the cause, criticizing the high internal support and external farm subsidy levels being maintained by the EC. The Cairns Group also denounced the United States for its recent growth in farm support and export subsidy spending. The emergence of this group guarantees a more vocal opposition in Geneva to business as usual on agriculture. Cairns Group criticism of the United States may actually be tactically convenient, if it helps the American delegation assume something closer to a middle position in the spectrum of argument, and if it helps weaken the futile polarization of most U.S.-EC conflicts on agriculture.

On the negative side, unfortunately, there are several factors working against success in the current round. First, in the ongoing negotiations the United States is not just a demandeur on agriculture. The U.S. trading position in all products has recently undergone a massive deterioration, requiring American negotiators to be the major demandeur on almost all the other issues under discussion in Geneva, including trade in services, investment, and intellectual property rights. The implications of this new role for the United States are that the strategy used in the Kennedy Round (and even then unsuccessfully), of offering trade concessions in other areas in order to get a better deal for U.S. agriculture, will probably not even be available. The United States has gone to Geneva this time with urgent demands to make across-the-board, and with even less than before to offer in return.

Conceivably, the United States could use its recently enlarged overall trade imbalance to gain a tactical advantage in the current round. As a large net importer in most nonagricultural sectors, the United States can now threaten a great deal of damage by lapsing further into protectionism. Threats of increased protection on the industrial side could perhaps be used to seek foreign concessions on the agriculture side. This high-risk strategy is favored by some agriculturists (especially by those who do not want to make any concessions of their own), but it will be both difficult and dangerous to pursue in the current GATT round, since both the content of U.S. trade legislation and the sector-by-sector organization of the GATT negotiations are biased against any kind of cross-sectoral bargaining.[26]

As a second negative factor, strictly within the farm sector, U.S. negotiators still lack adequate authority to offer the credible nontariff concessions necessary to win concessions from others in return. Under Section 102 of the 1974 Trade Act—which will expire in January 1988 if it is not extended—NTB agreements become U.S. law only if Congress subsequently passes implementing legislation.[27] Even when this legislation can be considered on a "fast track," and with no amendments allowed, doubts about the likelihood of congressional approval can slow down bargaining in Geneva. U.S. negotiators have said that "this time everything is on the table," and optimists hope that they will be able to gain concessions from the EC by offering to give up such things as the 1955 GATT waiver on quantitative import restrictions. EC negotiators, however, will not only be weighing the limited trade value to their own farmers of such an offer; they will also be assessing the uncertain ability of U.S. negotiators to persuade their own potentially affected domestic dairy, sugar, beef, and peanut interests to go along with the bargain.

Finally, a negotiated agreement on agriculture may be more difficult in the current round because of a EC demand that the discussions include not only border measures which distort trade directly, such as EC export restitutions, but also domestic farm subsidies which have an indirect effect on trade, such as U.S. target-price deficiency payments. The 1986 Punta del Este Ministerial Declaration, at EC insistence, stipulated reductions in "all direct and indirect subsidies, and other measures affecting directly or indirectly agricultural trade." The recent growth in U.S. target-price deficiency payments to farmers, which are undeniably an indirect production subsidy, will leave U.S. domestic farm policy open to difficult EC challenges on this score. The result could once again be a deadlock, since U.S. negotiators in Geneva still lack any clear authority from Congress to make commitments on domestic target-price reductions.

What happens to the rest of the Uruguay Round if such a deadlock should emerge on agriculture? If U.S. farm interests begin to sense that the GATT process is failing them once again, congressional support for important bargains that might be reached in other sectors could be jeopardized. At the very least, U.S. farm interests will be required to show exceptional patience, since few complete results are expected in the current round before the 1990s. With the prospects for a strong U.S. agricultural export recovery problematic in the meantime, this patience will be hard to secure. Efforts to bring back some "early harvest" for U.S. farmers, perhaps through a cosmetic subsidy "freeze" agreement, will become tactically very tempting.

Strategies for the United States in the Uruguay Round

Given this mix of new advantages and new difficulties, what agricultural liberalization strategy should U.S. negotiators pursue in the Uruguay Round? At least four alternative grand strategies might be considered:

1. A *comprehensive conversion* of existing agricultural trade barriers into customs tariffs, which could then be frozen and reduced through the use of conventional GATT negotiating techniques.

2. A *comprehensive measurement* of all existing agricultural subsidies, nation-by-nation, followed by a multilateral agreement first to freeze and then later to reduce those subsidies.

3. A *piecemeal tightening* of existing GATT rules on the most illiberal agricultural trade practices, including export subsidies and import restrictions, plus a strengthening of dispute-settlement procedures.

4. A *commodity-specific bilateral deal*, either with the EC or Japan, negotiated either with or without any fundamental change in existing GATT obligations.

The first of these alternatives—converting all nontariff farm trade barriers to tariffs, as a prelude to an across-the-board freeze and then reductions—was actually proposed to the GATT Committee on Trade in Agriculture (CTA) by U.S. delegates in February 1985. This radical approach would end the special treatment traditionally granted to agriculture in GATT, and supposedly make agricultural trade barriers more transparent and easier for GATT negotiators to reduce in an equitable fashion. But the technical and political problems associated with making such a radical conversion to tariffs would bring the momentum of any negotiation to a halt. Converting all existing NTBs to uniform tariffs—including all U.S. and Japanese import quotas, all EC variable import levies, and all Australian and Canadian state-trading instruments—would probably prove even more difficult in GATT than a direct assault on those barriers in their present form.

This U.S. "tariff-regime" proposal was constructed in 1985 as an improvised international accompaniment to the administration's equally radical 1985 domestic farm bill proposal, which both parties in Congress immediately pronounced "dead on arrival." The tariff-regime proposal in GATT did not fare any better. The EC led a broadly based rejection of the U.S. plan inside the CTA, arguing correctly that a less radical starting point would be needed if any progress at all was to be made.

A second Uruguay Round strategy—and one which has recently gained favor with some U.S. negotiators—is to allow today's farm trade instruments to continue functioning in their current form, while agreeing upon a comprehensive method for measuring those instruments in terms of their tariff or "subsidy equivalents." A subsequent agreement could then be made to cap and eventually to reduce those subsidy equivalents, over time, in a multilateral fashion. Parallel multilateral efforts could then be undertaken to reduce excess production capacity and to dispose of existing surplus stocks.

What is needed at the outset to pursue this strategy is an acceptable method of measuring agricultural "subsidy equivalents." One sophisticated technique for measuring both producer-subsidy equivalents (PSEs) and consumer-subsidy equivalents (CSEs) was developed for the United Nations Food and Agriculture Organization (FAO) more than a decade ago. This technique, which has more recently been adopted by the OECD, measures PSEs as a ratio, with the total value of all *income transfers to farmers caused by policy* in the numerator and *total agricultural income* in the denominator. The higher the ratio, the heavier the policy subsidy to producer income.

PSEs are more comprehensive as a subsidy yardstick than a simple ratio between internal and border prices. This is because income can be transferred to farmers through many policy means which may not directly affect commodity prices (including input or marketing subsidies, publicly sponsored agricultural research, and some forms of direct cash payments). Even for the most able economist, translating such diverse policies into quantified "subsidy equivalents" can be a complicated and contentious exercise, but a determined multilateral effort to master this problem, originally mandated within OECD in 1982, is now bearing fruit. PSE measurements generated by this OECD study, based on 1979–81 data were finally unveiled, after much delay and amid continuing controversy, in May 1987. They have yet to be officially accepted by all the OECD governments involved, but they have earned considerable respect within the research community. An updated sample of these PSE measurements, put out by the U.S. Department of Agriculture and based on 1982–84 data, is reproduced in Table 5.

Note that in 1982–84, Japanese farmers received by far the most generous ratio of subsidized income, with a 72 percent weighted-average. The EC was next with a 33 percent weighted-average. Canada, New Zealand, and the United States were grouped at 22–23 percent, and Australia was at the bottom of the list with only 9 percent.

A GATT strategy to "bind" and then reduce these existing subsidy equivalents might have several advantages. While placing an upper limit on overall income transfers to farmers, such a freeze would not prevent individual nations from using whatever specific instruments of income transfer their individual policy institutions might require. They could use internal or border measures as they might choose, as long as the total subsidy equivalent remained capped. Also, binding a PSE—as opposed to fixing a quantitative market share—leaves countries some opportunity to continue adjusting actual trade patterns to shifting comparative advantages, thus promoting economic efficiency.[28] An overall subsidy cap has the added plus of being intuitively easy to grasp, at least in concept. This is no small advantage in building necessary political support for an agreement. A subsidy cap also seems a well-tailored short-run device to counter the greatest immediate risk of an escalating U.S.-EC export subsidy war.

It is not surprising, therefore, to find considerable support for this overall subsidy freeze and reduction approach, using either PSEs or some less complicated summary measure of policy support. Both Canada and Australia have proposed first a freeze and then a reduction in the gap between each nation's internal and border prices, usually referred to as the level of "nominal protection." One respected U.S. expert has proposed a freeze in national price subsidies, and in the quantity of production receiving subsidies.[29]

Table 5

Weighted-Average PSE and Major Sources of Assistance, 1982–84

Country and region	Weighted-average PSE	Major sources of assistance to producers			
		Grains and oilseeds	Dairy	Livestock	Sugar
	Percent				
Japan	72[1]	Grains: State trading Oilseeds: Deficiency payments	Price support through government stock-holding and border restriction; also some deficiency payments	Beef: Quotas, tariff, and domestic price stabilization scheme Pork: Variable levy Poultry: Tariff	Tariffs, surcharges, and rebates
EC	33	Grains: Variable import levies and export subsidies Oilseeds: Deficiency payments	Variable import levies, export subsidies, and government purchases	Variable import levies and export subsidies	Variable import levies and export subsidies
Canada	22	Wheat and barley: Transport subsidies and income stabilization payments Corn: Tariff Oilseeds: Transport subsidies and income stabilization payments	Domestic price support (maintained with import quotas) and direct payments	Beef and pork: Tariffs, inspection services Poultry: Quota, price support, and tariff	Tariff, stabilization payments

Table 5 (Cont'd)

Country and region	Weighted-average PSE	Major sources of assistance to producers			
		Grains and oilseeds	Dairy	Livestock	Sugar
	Percent				
New Zealand	23	Marketing board controlled trade and set prices	Interest rate concessions (farm improvement loans and loans to marketing board)	Direct income payment	Not applicable
United States	22	Grains: Deficiency payments, PIK entitlements, CCC inventory operations, and commodity loans Oilseeds: CCC inventory operations and commodity loans	Price supports maintained by tariffs, quotas, and government purchases	Beef: Tariff Other: General (R&D, inspection, etc.)	Price supports and quotas
Australia	9	Domestic consumption pricing	Domestic consumption pricing	Input subsidies and inspection services	Domestic consumption pricing

[1]Excludes citrus. When citrus is added, weighted PSE is 65 percent.

Source: U.S. Department of Agriculture, Economic Research Service, "Government Intervention in Agriculture: Measurement, Evaluation and Implications for Trade Negotiations," _Foreign Agricultural Economic Report_, no. 229 (April 1987), p. 33.

Acknowledging the intuitive appeal of a PSE freeze and reduction strategy, several pitfalls must be kept in mind. First, any PSE freeze which does not promptly lead to significant reductions could be an empty victory, since present price levels and subsidy ratios are already much too high. A freeze would lock in currently inequitable levels of permitted protection country-by-country, and it would imply no change in current production and trade distortions. Under a freeze, neither the high U.S. target prices (which were frozen by law in 1985) nor the high EC CAP prices (also effectively frozen, in ECU terms), which are helping to generate the current production surplus, would be forced to come down. Unfortunately, price or subsidy levels that are merely frozen can generate increasing production and trade distortions, as agricultural productivity continues to increase.

Even if we assume that an actual subsidy reduction could be negotiated, some problems with the "comprehensive-measurement" approach would still remain. First, the apparent equity of any comprehensive subsidy measurement scheme, even with reductions, would immediately be undone by fluctuating currency exchange rates. Nations with depreciating currencies would experience automatic reductions in their internal-to-border price ratio, giving them more leeway to subsidize farmers, while nations with appreciating currencies would experience the opposite effect.

Measures such as PSEs and internal-to-border price ratios are also less than ideal because they misjudge the actual impact on production—and hence on trade—of some internal farm "subsidy" instruments. In the United States, some subsidy payments to farmers (deficiency payments) are conditioned upon the removal of land from production. Conventional PSE measurements do not factor in this implied restraint on production, and as a result they systematically overestimate the trade-distorting consequences of some important U.S. farm subsidy programs. PSEs also fail to capture the reduced incentive to production that occurs when subsidy payments to farmers are "decoupled" from price-support guarantees. Decoupling, which tends to reduce both production and consumption distortions, should be promoted in GATT, rather than discouraged or treated neutrally in this fashion. A much better way to encourage decoupling would be to build an agreement around measures of "producer-incentive" equivalents, or PIEs.[30] The sweeping U.S. proposal to GATT in July 1987 seems to make a conceptual move in this direction, since it allows some income supports which are production neutral, and targets for eventual elimination only those subsidy programs which distort production, prices and trade. Whether or not this conceptual shift will be acceptable to those in the OECD who until now have followed the more conventional PSE approach remains to be seen.

To step back from such quibbles, it may prove difficult to negotiate a binding agreement based on any set of technical measurements which only a handful of highly trained economists can claim to understand. Politicians will have doubts about surrendering their sovereign power to a technical formula which they have had little or no role in designing. It would also prove difficult to enforce such a binding agreement on overall levels of support. Agricultural policy officials wishing to increase the level of support they provide to their farmers will be able to find loopholes in any PSE formula, much as good tax lawyers find loopholes in the Internal Revenue Code. Artful ways of repackaging or remeasuring subsidies will proliferate.[31]

Measuring the subsidy equivalent of national agricultural policies is an extremely useful exercise in the OECD and in GATT even though it may never become the basis for a formal agreement. The "shaming" effect of having comprehensive subsidy measurements on the table constantly reminds negotiators that all nations are implicated in the distortions that plague agriculture, thus encouraging joint efforts to remedy the situation. Agricultural negotiators should be wary, however, of spending too much time working in this new realm of subsidy equivalents. They should save some time and energy for the negotiation of much needed improvements in the existing body of GATT rules governing agriculture. The subsidy-equivalent approach, at the very least, should not be allowed to displace or to weaken these existing GATT rules. The concept of blending all subsidy practices into a single measure, if it became the practice in GATT, would weaken the existing GATT distinction between subsidies which discriminate directly against foreign producers, such as quantitative import restrictions and export subsidies, and less offensive subsidies which do not, such as decoupled farm income-support payments.

A third strategic approach to the Uruguay Round would be to build on existing GATT rules and distinctions by negotiating such things as tighter language in Article XVI on export subsidies, improved market access guarantees in Article XI, and better dispute-settlement procedures. This "piecemeal-improvements" approach lacks popular political appeal because it promises no sudden revolutionary breakthrough. Even if tightened considerably, today's GATT rules on agricultural trade will not be able to provide the conceptual basis for anything approaching comprehensive liberalization. By building on existing GATT rules, however, at least two advantages can be gained. First, a piecemeal-improvements strategy would ensure at least some forward progress on agriculture in the current negotiating round. This is important not only for agriculture, but also for other U.S. sectoral interests that might be hurt if the Uruguay Round were to attempt too much and then collapse in failure. Second, there is the unquestionable advantage of reaffirming GATT's existing rules and procedures which provide a valuable set of inhibitions against *backward* progress into even greater farm trade protectionism.

GATT may not be a proven instrument for securing ambitious upside liberal gains, but its rules are often a useful means for holding in check those nations which want even more farm protection. One example is the role which GATT has played thus far in preserving access to the EC market for U.S. sales of soybeans, soybean meal, and corn gluten feed. As noted earlier, free entry of these nongrain feed ingredients is granted to the United States by virtue of the zero-duty bindings that the EC conceded at the end of the Dillon Round. According to GATT rules (Article XXVIII), once such a "binding" has been given it cannot be taken away without an offer of acceptable compensation, so as to preserve the existing balance of concessions. If adequate compensation is not provided, retaliation is explicitly permitted. This requirement for compensation also applies if measures are adopted (such as an internal tax, or a preferential arrangement with another supplier) that might reduce the commercial value of a tariff binding.

When the EC originally made its concession on free entry of nongrain feeds twenty-five years ago, it did not realize how significant it would prove to be. The subsequent embrace of a highly protectionist CAP cereals regime eventually made the purchase of U.S. nongrain feeds extremely attractive to the EC livestock industry, and so duty-free U.S. sales of soybeans and corn gluten feed to the Community expanded rapidly. In part thanks to GATT rules, those within the EC who wanted to close this loophole and "complete the CAP," by placing duties or quotas on grain substitute imports, were successfully deterred. When in 1983 the EC Commission recommended an internal consumption tax on nondairy fats and oils, American trade officials sent strong warnings that the United States would have every right, under GATT rules, to retaliate. These warnings, together with internal objections from Europe's own oilseed-crushing industry, persuaded the Council, at least on that occasion, not to go forward with the tax. EC efforts to put a cap on duty-free U.S. corn gluten sales have also been usefully constrained, at least in part, by GATT rules. When the Community at one point proposed to cap the duty-free import of U.S. corn gluten feed, it felt obliged to proceed cautiously, by offering to negotiate compensation strictly according to GATT rules. When the United States explained that the compensation being offered was not adequate, this initiative was effectively put in check. As mentioned previously, EC willingness to provide partial compensation to U.S. agriculture for market access lost due to the 1986 Community enlargement was also attributable, at least in part, to GATT norms and procedures.

U.S. officials anticipating a continuing farm trade struggle with the European Community (as indicated in early 1987 by the ominous revival of an EC fats and oils tax proposal) should not dismiss the protective value of existing GATT rules and procedures. They may not provide a promising conceptual basis for the complete liberalization of agriculture, but then neither the EC nor Japan is ever likely to accept total liberalization as a legitimate objective in GATT or anywhere else. U.S. negotiators will get nowhere by ignoring this reality. They will search for opportunities in GATT to make progress where possible through piecemeal improvements.

As a first step in this direction, in view of the recently disruptive U.S.-EC export subsidy competition, urgent attention should be paid to tightening the existing Subsidies Code. Several improvements could be considered. First, to help discipline subsidy abusers, a more detailed description of the "normal market conditions" being used at present by GATT panels as a point of reference could be negotiated. Second, language could be added to lighten the current burden to "prove causality" when bringing a case of market distortion against a subsidy abuser. Third, language could also be included to clarify the context—national or global—in which "equitable shares" are to be calculated. Finally, to improve dispute-settlement procedures, a provision could be considered to permit retaliation on the basis of a GATT panel finding alone if the GATT Council does not adopt the finding within a specified period. Lessons have been learned from the dispute-settlement disappointments experienced since the Tokyo Round, and the Uruguay Round presents negotiators with an important opportunity to profit from and to apply these lessons.

The United States must be aware that if these efforts to constrain export subsidies are successful, the EC will find itself—at least in the short run—with the need to absorb more of its agricultural surplus within its home market. This will increase the temptation to cut back even more rapidly on existing foreign imports. An isolated effort to solve the export subsidy problem, in other words, could intensify market access difficulties. Accordingly, the United States should also use the current round to negotiate, in Article XI, more secure and more equitable rules guaranteeing market access. For example, the variable import levies employed by the EC do not violate current GATT rules because they are not quantitative restrictions. In order to check any expanded abuse of this loophole, the United States might seek an extension of Article XI to cover all *new* government interventions (including increases in domestic support prices and subsidies) that threaten to reduce traditional import shares. This would not be an easy extension to negotiate because it would require agreement on a base period, and since access guarantees might have to be provided by quotas (for which foreign suppliers might ideally offer competitive bids). To make progress in this area the United States might also have to concede something on market access in return—perhaps its 1955 GATT waiver.

Beyond piecemeal improvements in the generalized rules and procedures of GATT, U.S. negotiators might also use the Uruguay Round as a setting in which to seek any number of bilateral or commodity-specific agricultural trade agreements, such as those reached with Japan during the Tokyo Round. For example, the EC will probably be looking for ways to "complete the CAP" by removing the zero-duty binding on nongrain feed imports that it accepted in the Dillon Round. The United States might be tempted to agree if it receives a concession in return, such as an agreed limit on EC cereals prices, or export restitutions, or export market shares, or perhaps a new binding on EC oilseed self-sufficiency levels. By one line of argument, the longer the United States chooses to delay such an ad hoc deal, the less the zero-duty binding will be worth given the rapid growth in subsidized oilseeds production inside the Community.[32]

There might also be a range of deals to consider which do not involve the binding, including multilateral crop acreage or dairy herd reductions, or, conceivably, EC cereals policy restraints in exchange for U.S. dairy policy restraints.[33] An ideal ad hoc bargain, given current world stock conditions, might be a formal or informal agreement between the United States and the EC to reduce domestic cereals production incentives. The United States could promise its best efforts to reduce domestic target prices, perhaps by 10 to 20 percent over a specified period, in return for an EC commitment to exercise parallel domestic cereals price or production restraints. Responsible officials in both Washington and Brussels are currently trying to find internal political support for just such changes. This support might be more forthcoming if expectations can be established, through GATT, that foreign competitors will be exercising price and production restraints at the same time. A commodity-specific U.S.-EC bargain on price reductions and production restraints will not be as appealing either to economists, or to multilateral rule-making purists, as an overall subsidy cap or reduction. Since it would immediately bind against existing domestic farm policies, it would also be more difficult to negotiate. For precisely this reason, however, it would also be more valuable than a cosmetic subsidy freeze.[34]

If GATT negotiations can be used as a setting in which to negotiate commodity-specific agreements which are genuinely trade expanding, there should be no reason for U.S. negotiators to hesitate. Care should be taken, however, to avoid illiberal commodity-specific agreements designed to "manage trade" in ways that reduce competition. The danger to U.S. agriculture of entering into such agreements will be discussed in the chapter that follows.

It is often noted that professional athletes do their best when "playing within their capabilities." U.S. farm trade negotiators will do best in Geneva if they play within GATT's capabilities. We have to hope, in this regard, that they will not use up too much negotiating time in Geneva advancing their far-fetched proposal to eliminate all production and trade distorting subsidies before the end of the century. This proposal goes too far beyond the terms of the Punta del Este Declaration, and too far beyond any agreement yet considered seriously in the OECD. Moreover, by the time this proposal was offered, in July 1987, it had for all practical purposes already been rejected, by the EC and Japan, at the Venice Economic Summit. This proposal also invites criticism because it greatly exaggerates the amount of policy reform that the U.S. Congress is currently willing to accept. It is likely to be received abroad as the ideological parting statement of a lame duck U.S. administration, rather than a foundation for serious negotiations.

GATT can become a useful arena in which to help fix farm trade if the lessons of past failure are kept properly in mind. Errors were made in the past by those who ignored the differences between agricultural trade and industrial trade, and by those who rushed to Geneva without first securing adequate negotiating authority from affected domestic farm producer interests. The essential prelude to a successful negotiation in Geneva must be a high-priority domestic negotiation between trade officials and congressional agricultural committees. Without a prior bargain on policy reform intentions at home, there will be nothing available for negotiators to give in Geneva, and hence nothing available to gain.

Notes

1. IIASA, *Towards Free Trade in Agriculture, op. cit.*, Table 6.14.
2. Ibid., Table 6.14 and Table 5.2.
3. See Johnson, Hemmi, and Lardinois, *Agricultural Policy and Trade, op. cit.*, p. 45.
4. "Level Field: Agricultural Subsidies Would be Jointly Cut Under U.S. Trade Plan," *Wall Street Journal*, April 7, 1987, p. 1.
5. Letter from Daniel G. Amstutz, Undersecretary for International Affairs and Commodity Programs, U.S. Department of Agriculture, *Choices*, (Fourth Quarter 1986), p. 38.
6. *Ministerial Declaration on the Uruguay Round*, Punta del Este, Uruguay, September 1986.
7. U.S. International Trade Commission, "Review of the Effectiveness of Trade Dispute Settlement Under the GATT and the Tokyo Round Agreements," Washington, December 1985. Unfortunately, many of the "most contentious" disputes have concerned agriculture, including five complaints brought specifically by the United States against the Common Agricultural Policy of the EC.
8. Whenever "any article or articles are being or are practically certain to be imported into the United States under such conditions and in such quantities as to render or tend to render ineffective or materially interfere with" any U.S. farm program. See Johnson, Hemmi, and Lardinois, *Agricultural Policy and Trade, op. cit.*, p. 66.
9. See Statement of Alan Woods before U.S. Senate Committee on Agriculture, Nutrition, and Forestry, July 29, 1986.
10. The standard practice was for the leading buyer of a product to negotiate reciprocal concessions directly with the leading supplier. These concessions would then be generalized to all contracting parties of the GATT. In the first round of trade talks in GATT in 1947, the twenty-three participants arrived at 45,000 concessions or agreements in this fashion.
11. See John A. Schnittker, "Reflections on Trade and Agriculture" in *Essays in Honour of Thorkil Kristensen* (Paris, Organization for

Economic Cooperation and Development, 1970), p. 264. Schnittker provides a candid description of the Kennedy Round negotiating experience, from the vantage point of a ranking official within the U.S. Department of Agriculture at the time.

12. Harald B. Malmgren, *International Economic Peacekeeping in Phase II* (New York: Quadrangle Books, 1972), pp. 120–123.

13. See Schnittker, "Reflections on Trade and Agriculture," *op. cit.,* p. 266.

14. I.M. Destler, *Making Foreign Economic Policy* (Washington: Brookings Institution, 1980), p. 176.

15. Ibid., pp. 176–78.

16. See I.M. Destler, *American Trade Politics: System Under Stress* (Washington, Institute for International Economics, 1986), p. 64.

17. Foreign governments in the Tokyo Round were unlikely to respond to any nontariff farm trade concessions that U.S. negotiators might try to offer without explicit congressional authority, because they had been burned once already in the Kennedy Round when concessions that they had accepted on the American selling price (ASP) system were subsequently not implemented by Congress.

18. Pietro S. Nivola, "The New Protectionism: U.S. Trade Policy in Historical Perspective," *Political Science Quarterly*, vol. 101, no. 4 (1986), p. 596.

19. Any country that has signed the Code can notify the Committee of Signatories that it believes another country has provided a subsidy that is inconsistent with the Code. Following this notification, the the country alleged to be providing the subsidy and the affected country enter a consultation period. If no solution to the problem can be found through consultations, the matter can be referred to the Committee for conciliation. Where this fails, a panel of experts may be appointed to investigate. The panel prepares a report for consideration by the Committee, and if the Committee believes a subsidy inconsistent with the Code has been granted, it will recommend that the subsidy be eliminated. If the subsidy is not eliminated, the Code empowers the Committee to authorize retaliatory counter-measures against the subsidizing country to pressure the country into compliance. See *A Preface to Trade*, The Office of the U.S. Trade Representative, Executive Office of the President, Washington, 1982, p. 93.

20. See Fred H. Sanderson, Statement to the Subcommittee on Foreign Agriculture of Senate Committee on Agriculture, August 5,

1986, p. 13. Sanderson argues that a "bolder" panel might have found enough "negotiating history" to support the selection of a three-year period immediately prior to the adoption of the Code as a basis for defining the EC's equitable share.

21. In August 1986, a complicated bilateral agreement was reached in which the EC promised to offer some greater market access to American citrus products and almonds, in return for a U.S. promise not to challenge the legality of European citrus preferences in GATT, plus some other concessions on imports of European olives, olive oil, anchovies, paprika, capers, fermented cider, and some cheeses. In addition, both sides made a commitment to negotiate acceptable pasta subsidy levels while leaving aside the disputed GATT legality of those subsidies. Also included in this remarkable 1986 package of non-GATT agreements was U.S. implementation of a previously negotiated increase in quotas on imports of EC semi-finished steel.

22. An editorial in *The Economist* argued that on principle this was a bad agreement: "Quotas are the most destructive sort of market protection. Bilateral deals tear the basic fabric of the world's trading system. If trade peace means a proliferation of bilateral quota agreements, it will be little better than outright trade war—a depressing outlook for the new Uruguay Round of GATT talks, which is supposed to herald real progress towards the goal of freer trade." *The Economist*, January 31, 1987, p. 14.

23. The expanded use of export subsidies was immediately advocated by U.S. farm producers—and eventually endorsed by U.S. trade negotiators—as a "tactical tool" to speed progress in the Uruguay Round. And protection-minded senators from farm states have already introduced legislation that would mandate an across-the-board "marketing loan" (in effect, an extended deficiency payment) on all 1990 program crops if substantial progress has not been made in GATT by 1989.

24. By one rough estimate, multilateral OECD liberalization could help reduce the drop in domestic U.S. agricultural price ratios to just 2 percent, only one-third as large as the 6 percent drop that might occur if the United States were to liberalize alone. See IIASA, *Towards Free Trade in Agriculture, op. cit.*, Tables 5.2, 6.4, and 6.14.

25. Included in the Cairns Group are Argentina, Australia, Brazil, Canada, Chile, Colombia, Fiji, Hungary, Indonesia, Malaysia, New Zealand, the Philippines, Thailand, and Uruguay.

26. For a more comprehensive discussion of cross-sectoral bargains

and negotiating timetables in the current round, see C. Michael Aho and Jonathan D. Aronson, *Trade Talks: America Better Listen!* (New York, Council on Foreign Relations, 1985), especially Chapter 2.

27. "U.S. Agricultural Trade Relations," Congressional Research Service Issue Brief, IB86056 (October 15, 1986), p. CRS-3.

28. Stefan Tangermann, "Approaches to Agricultural Trade Liberalization in the GATT" (Working Paper No. 4 for a Council on Foreign Relations study group on The Future of U.S. Agricultural Trade Policy, Washington, September 23, 1986.)

29. Dale E. Hathaway, *Agriculture and the GATT: Issues in a New Trade Round* (Washington: Institute for International Economics, 1987), forthcoming.

30. See Gordon C. Rausser and Brian D. Wright, "Alternative Strategies for Trade Policy Reform," California Agricultural Experiment Station, Giannini Foundation of Agricultural Economics, April 1987.

31. It is relatively easy for clever policy specialists to disguise an increase in overall subsidy levels. Early in 1987, for example, the House Agriculture Committee managed to add approximately $300 million to the U.S. Export-Enhancement Program simply by changing the cost-accounting standards used by the Department of Agriculture for valuing the CCC commodities being donated to that program.

32. M. Ann Tutwiler and George E. Rossmiller, "Negotiating Agriculture in the GATT: Getting What You Want" (Paper for the National Planning Association's Committee on Agriculture, Washington, April 4, 1987).

33. For one extensive review of such ad hoc commodity-specific GATT options, see Fred H. Sanderson, *Agricultural Trade Issues* (Washington: Council for U.S. International Trade Policy, 1987), forthcoming.

34. For a review of the impact on U.S. and EC agriculture of several different combinations of commodity-specific farm policy reforms, see Ulrich Koester, "Disharmonies in EC and U.S. Agricultural Policy Measures: A Summary," Draft Final Executive Summary, University of Kiel, Federal Republic of Germany, March 1987.

Three

How to Fix Farm Trade: Outside of GATT

A s we have seen, agricultural trade problems are extremely difficult to resolve in GATT, thus trade officials are tempted to look for ways to resolve their difficulties outside of GATT. At one extreme, they have tried to "manage" agricultural trade through market-fixing international commodity agreements. At another extreme, trade policymakers have attempted, at times, to use coercive instruments such as export subsidies and import restrictions to wage and to win an agricultural trade "war." In this chapter we shall review both the promise and the actual performance of these various cooperative and coercive international agricultural trade policy options outside of GATT. The considerable risks contained in both of these non-GATT options—including risks to the GATT process itself—will be found to outweigh the possibilities for substantial gain to U.S. agriculture. We shall conclude that a more helpful set of non-GATT farm policy initiatives are those now waiting to be taken at home, rather than abroad, in the area of further U.S. domestic farm policy reform.

Once we move our analysis outside of GATT, a wide range of strategic and tactical options suddenly become available. Outside of GATT, nondiscriminatory multilateral procedures do not have to be observed at all times, and genuine agricultural trade liberalization need not always be the ultimate objective. Cooperative multilateral procedures can be used to pursue *nonliberal* goals, such as the "management" of world farm markets through an international commodity agreement. Non-cooperative unilateral procedures could also be used to pursue liberalization through, for example, the waging of a coercive "farm trade war" against protectionists. Are any of these non-GATT policy options compatible with U.S. international agricultural trade interests, and with the success of agricultural trade negotiations in the current Uruguay Round?

The Management of International Commodity Trade

One of the most obvious ways to try to "fix" farm trade outside of GATT is to negotiate international commodity agreements specifying such things as the price at which products will be traded, the quantity of goods that each nation will buy or sell at that price, the surplus stocks that each country will carry, and the market share that each will maintain. Agreements of this kind to "manage" trade are in essence agreements *not to compete,* and as such they are at odds with the more liberal spirit of the GATT. For those who perceive destructive tendencies in liberal international farm trade competition, however, such agreements have long appeared to present a more "cooperative" alternative.

International commodity agreements (ICAs) to manage farm trade outside of GATT can be negotiated among just a few exporters, or among all exporters, or more broadly still among all exporters and all importers. Bringing exporters together with importers has been the preferred strategy of most ICA proponents over the years because of the implied sense of fairness to all. The United States, in fact, has participated in many such comprehensive international farm commodity agreements, the most famous being the International Wheat Agreement of 1933. A brief review of this experience reveals a great deal about the prospects for operating successful international commodity agreements today.[1]

Past Experience

1933 was a time, not unlike the present, of large world wheat surpluses. The United States took the lead (together with other exporters, such as Canada and Australia) in organizing the first International Wheat Agreement (IWA). This original agreement was designed to reduce fluctuations in world price and production through a multilateral contract which specified maximum and minimum prices at which participants were obliged to sell or purchase specified quantities of wheat. All exporting countries were also required to reduce planted area by 15 percent in the first two years. This production-control feature of the agreement was notably unsuccessful. Australian agricultural officials still remember—and no doubt resent—the fact that they were the only exporting nation to meet acreage-reduction obligations. When Argentina exceeded its export quota in the second year, the formal agreement temporarily collapsed.[2]

Following World War II, the agreement was frequently revived, renewed, and revised. Versions of the IWA required participating importers to import each year either a stipulated quantity (under the 1949–56 agreements) or a stipulated share (under agreements after 1959) of their total needs from exporting members, at prices within a specified range.[3] In the 1960s, some U.S. officials made tentative efforts to broaden the scope of this agreement to include coarse grains, but they ran into stiff opposition from U.S. domestic coarse grain producers, who have traditionally been more opposed than wheat growers to international price-fixing.

During the period 1949–67 when these postwar agreements were in effect, international wheat prices did remain remarkably stable. The largest variation in average annual prices from one year to the next was a 16 percent drop noted in 1967, just prior to the agreement's final collapse. It is important to realize, however, that only a small part of this price stability was the result of the agreement itself. The proportion of world trade covered by the agreement was actually declining during this period, to only 25 percent in the mid-1950s, because a number of importers had failed to renew their participation. International price stability was mostly a coincidental by-product of the willingness of the United States (together with Canada, in a "duopolistic" fashion) to support and stabilize commercial export prices through high domestic loan rates and through the carrying of disproportionately large domestic stocks.[4] No less important was the prevailing global macroeconomic environment of the 1950s and early

1960s, which was marked by strong and steady worldwide growth at fixed exchange rates under the still functioning Bretton Woods system.

The postwar International Wheat Agreement finally became unsustainable in the late 1960s, when the United States grew tired of propping up prices by carrying expensive domestic stocks, losing foreign commercial market shares in the process to less efficient foreign competitors. As a consequence, the United States decided to adopt a more aggressive export strategy in the mid-1960s, which included not only a program for lower commodity loan rates at home, but also the more lavish use of direct export subsidies abroad. A new wheat agreement was negotiated in 1967, but it collapsed within eighteen months under heavy downward market pressures when the United States, joined this time by Australia and France, failed to "protect" the price minimum. Only Canada, among the exporters, exercised discipline.

Following this experience, official U.S. interest in joining ICAs for major farm products declined noticeably. Avoiding such agreements was apparently confirmed as intelligent policy early in the 1970s, when U.S. agriculture found itself free to take maximum advantage of a sudden surge in foreign demand, through unconstrained growth in both its export prices and its export market share. So quickly did U.S. farm exports grow after 1972 that within two years practically all domestic surplus grain stocks were gone. At this unusual juncture, with world agricultural trade momentarily disrupted by high rather than low prices, the United States actually began to consider the value of another kind of international wheat agreement, one that would be designed to protect *consumers* as much as producers. Between 1975 and 1979 the United States took the lead, within the United Nations Conference for Trade and Development (UNCTAD) and the London-based International Wheat Council (IWC), in trying to negotiate a new international wheat agreement built around the creation and management of price-moderating national grain reserves. When world price levels subsequently became more reasonable, fears of a "world food crisis" passed and this effort collapsed as well.[5]

Even if these UNCTAD/IWC negotiations had produced a signed and ratified agreement to manage international stocks, there is little reason to believe that it could have functioned as planned in what eventually became a "post-food crisis" era of rapidly falling prices, a "post-Bretton Woods" era of fluctuating exchange rates and undisciplined macroeconomic policies, and a "post-détente" era of grain embargos (the USSR, the world's largest grain importer, had been an active participant in the UNCTAD/IWC negotiations). Even on its own terms, the draft agreement left plenty of room for misapplication—or non-application. In order to accommodate EC demands, the draft agreement had been built around a bewildering set of six separate rising and falling price trigger points, each linked to stock-management obligations which were so complex as to be—according to one assessment—"virtually incomprehensible."[6] The head of the U.S. delegation in the negotiations later testified that the terms of the agreement were "probably unworkable and certainly not negotiable in the UNCTAD framework."[7]

When a more "market-oriented" U.S. administration came to power in 1981, all efforts to negotiate broad ICAs to manage trade in agriculture came to a halt. Some might argue that this was bad timing, since it was also in 1981 that U.S. farm exports began their rapid decline, unprotected by any cooperative international agreement on trade volume or trade shares. In light of this painful experience, should the United States now reconsider the advantages of negotiating international agreements—either inside or outside of GATT—to "manage" farm trade?

Food importing countries can be expected to show little interest in a price-boosting international grains agreement so long as the low prices guaranteed by current market conditions continue. Importers, however, do not have to be included. Since it is the exporters—including those in both the United States and the EC—that are being damaged the most in today's depressed world farm markets, perhaps an agreement "not to compete" just among exporters might be sufficient. It could take the form of a promise not to undercut minimum prices, or it could be a commitment not to exceed maximum export quantities or market shares. If observed, such an agreement might free today's rival exporters from the commercial uncertainties (and the diplomatic tensions) that accompany trade competition. Of particular importance, it could also alleviate the heavy budget costs and trade distortions that accompany competitive export subsidies,

which usually nullify each another, thereby passing on un-
earned benefits only to importers. If a sweeping international
agreement to liberalize trade is unlikely to be reached any time
soon in GATT, then why not go for a second-best agreement to
manage trade, at least among exporters, outside of GATT?

A Word of Caution to the United States

If the United States were to set aside its objective of a liberal farm
trade solution which would benefit everyone, and opt instead
for a managed farm trade solution just in the interest of exporters, it would be running several large risks. First, there is the
danger of giving away any possibility for the future recovery of
U.S. agricultural export shares, which have decreased dramatically since 1981. Foreign export competitors would be in position
to use shrunken U.S. export shares as a basis for negotiating a
"managed trade" agreement permanently disadvantageous to
U.S. agriculture. Care must be taken not to freeze the unsatisfactory status quo.

Second, even if the formal terms of a managed trade agreement could be made attractive to U.S. agriculture, there is little
assurance that other exporters would be willing or able to comply with its terms. This being the case, the United States would
find itself in the uncomfortable position of sacrificing alone, once
again propping up export prices for its less disciplined foreign
competitors. This is not to say that other nations would enter a
managed trade agreement with a clear intent to cheat, but they
could discover that, once party to such an agreement, they are
unable to impose on their own farm sectors the production discipline necessary to comply. The key to any agricultural trade
management agreement under current world market conditions
would be production control, a burden which should be shared
equitably by all producers and exporters and especially by those
with high costs. Due to the tendencies inherent in the domestic
farm policies of most exporting nations today, this burden
would probably end up being shouldered almost entirely by the
United States.

The lessons of the 1980s are clear on this point. Whenever the
United States has exercised agricultural production restraint,
opportunistic competitors abroad have expanded their own pro-

duction and their own share of world exports at the expense of U.S. agriculture. This tendency showed itself most clearly in 1983, when the United States attempted to halt the costly accumulation of its own government-owned surplus grain stocks by paying farmers with those stocks (a payment "in kind" rather than in cash) to take land out of production. Under this Payment in Kind (PIK) program, the United States idled more cropland than all of Western Europe planted to crops. American wheat producers cut their harvested acreage by roughly 22 percent. U.S. corn production was cut (in part due to a 1983 drought as well as to the PIK program) by a massive 49 percent.

The price-firming effects of these American production cutbacks were unfortunately nullified by the offsetting, opportunistic response of most foreign competitors. The EC, which had been on the verge of running out of money for agricultural subsidy programs in 1983, was given some financial breathing space by higher prices and kept its full-production grain policies in place. Canada, Australia, and Argentina all boosted their wheat output. Their share of world wheat trade expanded, while the U.S. share continued in steep decline. Total U.S. wheat and coarse grain production fell by 38 percent under the PIK program, while the production of major export competitors such as Canada, Australia, Argentina, South Africa, and Thailand increased by 11 percent.[8] Overall, the United States set aside 77 million acres of land in 1983. Other countries responded by increasing their plantings by 63 million acres, thereby offsetting most of the American cutbacks.

Since U.S. commodity target prices remained high after PIK, it did not take long for the American surplus stocks to mount up again. Between 1983 and 1985, the U.S. share of total world wheat and coarse grain stocks increased from 44 percent up to 60 percent. By accumulating this disproportionate share of world stocks the United States was again firming up international prices for its less disciplined foreign competitors who, in response, increased their share of world wheat and coarse grain exports still more, from 46 percent up to 64 percent between 1981 and 1985.[9]

Among U.S. export competitors, it is usually the EC (and particularly France) which talks most about the need for a multilateral agreement to "manage trade." Yet the essence of EC strategy has been to take unilateral advantage whenever production restraint has been exercised by the United States. In grain markets, from 1978 through 1986, the United States took 109.8 million acres of its own wheat land out of production—more than the total acreage planted in France. In effect, the U.S. government was arranging for its own farmers *not* to produce the equivalent of 89 million tons of wheat. The French response was to expand its own surplus wheat production during this period by 70.5 million tons.[10] If it wishes to present itself to the United States as a credible partner in the joint management of world farm markets, the EC will first have to demonstrate a greater capacity to restrain its own farm production in times of slackening world demand.[11]

On the other hand, even if the EC were prepared to join the United States in a coordinated effort to firm up world farm prices, the result would only be an increase in the production and export incentives for Canada, Australia, Argentina, and numerous other equally aggressive competitors. More than 100 nations around the world produce wheat, many for export. With so many other active players in the market, it would be commercial suicide for the United States and the EC, which together account for only about 27 percent of world wheat production, to enter into a bilateral agreement "not to compete."

The final disadvantage for the United States to consider when contemplating market management schemes is the risk of losing the absolute competitive advantage which U.S. agriculture ought to enjoy in world farm trade. Between 1970 and 1982, the average productivity of U.S. farmland increased by a phenomenal 39 percent versus an overall 27 percent in the rest of the world. The average productivity of U.S. agricultural labor rose by 97 percent, compared to a 22 percent increase in other countries. Even the average product per unit of machinery increased in the United States while falling in the rest of the world. This higher U.S. productivity growth has come from a natural abundance of well-watered land; well-educated and highly skilled farmers using the best technology available; relatively efficient markets; and well-developed infrastructure and support industries.[12] There is no end in sight to this implied U.S. capacity to continue offering more farm products to the world's customers at prices lower than most of the competition. In fact, U.S. agriculture is now about to experience yet another period of exceptionally rapid productivity growth—forecast at annual rates as high as 2.4 percent—thanks in part to breakthroughs in biotechnology and genetic engineering.

Rapid productivity growth is often viewed as a domestic political liability, because socially difficult resource adjustments (including the movement of human labor out of farming) will usually follow, and as an international commercial liability, because of the recently sluggish growth in international demand for farm products at any price. This view is wrongheaded and self-defeating. In every other sector of the U.S. economy, rapid productivity growth is for good reason a highly sought after objective. It is ironic that in agriculture it should be considered a "problem." Agricultural productivity growth in the United States should be eagerly pursued, and more effectively used, as a means to create wealth more quickly at home while winning markets away from less productive competitors abroad.

U.S. agricultural productivity growth becomes a threat only if it is not employed. Productive domestic farm operators cash in on their competitiveness by underpricing their less efficient foreign competitors. If this opportunity is taken away from them, either by rigid domestic farm commodity programs or by international commodity agreements, their adjustment problems will become worse rather than better. In a "managed" world marketplace, more of the productivity growth of U.S. agriculture would have to be absorbed domestically, which would mean an even more rapid downsizing of the U.S. farm sector. Rapid agricultural productivity growth, which is an unbeatable commercial asset in a competitive international trade environment, becomes a liability once agreements are reached with other producers "not to compete." If the United States yields to other producers by allowing them to dictate the terms on which world farm trade will be managed, then a competitive advantage that ought to be available to the United States will be permanently lost.

In those farm markets where the United States is likely to remain a low-cost producer—such as corn, soybeans, and wheat—there is no commercial advantage at all to be gained from "cooperation" with higher-cost producers abroad.[13] It is the low-cost producer that suffers by giving away opportunities for future market and export growth. In those markets where the United States is a potentially successful competitor, strategies for liberal competition should be instinctively preferred over schemes for illiberal cooperation or "trade management."

Waging a Farm Trade War

Some who agree that it is futile to try to manage agricultural trade with illiberal foreign competitors outside of GATT will argue that the United States has no choice left but to beat those competitors at their own game. It should "fight fire with fire," by waging and winning a farm trade war. If foreign competitors, such as the EC, use illiberal import restrictions and export subsidies to boost their market share at the expense of the United States, then America should respond in kind with twice the measure. The "deeper pockets" of the federal government, plus a strong position in the world market, are trusted to provide America with an overpowering advantage in the use of such rough tactics. All that prevents the United States from regaining a larger share of world agricultural trade, according to this view, is a misplaced faith in GATT principles and an outdated habit of self-imposed restraint.

Some who support the trade war option recognize that sizable budget costs, and perhaps even some U.S. agricultural trade losses, might have to be absorbed in the short run. Others, however, believe that a satisfactory settlement could be reached short of a full-scale trade war, and at a relatively low cost. The mere threat of such a war—if made credible through the escalating use of ever tougher U.S. trade tactics—would be enough to force prompt changes in the illiberal policies of competitors abroad. Still others will claim that they want greater budget authority for export subsidies simply as a "bargaining chip" to use in negotiating a better deal for U.S. agriculture, either inside or outside of GATT.[14]

Until now, the U.S. government has stopped short of launching an all-out farm trade war against its foreign competitors.

Total U.S. spending on farm export subsidies is still only a fraction of total EC spending on farm export restitutions. This frustrates many in the U.S. farm community who believe their government is being too prudent. As it turns out, however, there is ample reason for caution. An examination of the current order of battle reveals that U.S. taxpayers, followed quickly by some U.S. farm exporters, would be among the first casualties if a full-scale farm trade war ever broke out.

Handicaps for the United States

There are at least four reasons why the United States would find itself at a relative disadvantage if it were ever to launch a full-scale international farm trade war. First, in any across-the-board export subsidy contest the United States would enter the competition with much larger existing foreign markets to defend. Second, the total budget cost to the United States of an export subsidy war would be much greater because of the way in which its domestic farm programs operate. Third, the United States is currently handicapped because its "deeper pockets" for waging an export subsidy competition have recently been emptied. Finally, some of America's most threatening foreign competitors—such as the EC—are still large importers of U.S. farm products and could retaliate with disproportionately damaging bilateral import restrictions. Each of these important handicaps deserves examination.

In a farm trade war, it does not help the United States to be the world's largest exporter of agricultural products. Large exporters are in fact at greater risk because they have more to lose. For example, if the United States were to enter a serious wheat export subsidy war with the EC, it would enter at a strategic disadvantage because it would begin with much larger existing foreign wheat markets to defend. Total U.S. wheat exports have shrunk badly in recent years, to as little as 25 million tons, but this is still roughly 10 million tons larger than total EC wheat exports. If an export subsidy war escalates, both the United States and the EC will be able to target any foreign market they choose, beginning most probably with those foreign markets currently held by the adversary. The United States, which still enjoys a larger volume of existing foreign sales, will have to spend more simply to protect these sales from EC subsidy encroachment. Just to stay even in world wheat markets—that is, simply to hold on to its currently unsatisfactory foreign market share—the United States might have to outspend the Community by as much as 50 percent in a full-scale export subsidy war.

Second, since the U.S. farm program budget is responsive to falling world prices both internally and at the border, the United States would not only have to spend more on subsidies abroad; it would also have to spend more on farm programs at home. An escalating export subsidy war would unfold as follows: world commodity prices would decline; U.S. domestic farm market prices would consequently drop; and, as a result, the budget cost of national farm programs would increase through larger target-price deficiency payments and more commodity loan forfeitures. Other exporters, such as the EC, would not suffer this double budget hardship because they do not let falling world market prices cross their borders, which cause an increase in domestic farm program costs. They have instruments, such as variable import levies, which maintain high and stable internal commodity price levels. For the EC, the result of falling world prices is a larger hidden cost to consumers, but no second budget burden on taxpayers.

Another reason why the United States would be handicapped in any expensive export subsidy war today is the overstrained condition of the domestic farm budget. It used to be said that the United States would be able to enter an export subsidy competition against smaller foreign governments with the advantage of having "deeper pockets." This might have been true just a few years ago, but today America's export subsidy pockets are practically empty, in part due to the high cost of its many lavish *domestic* farm programs. Between 1981 and 1985, the federal government spent an unprecedented $60 billion on farm price- and income-support programs. In 1986, farm program expenses were originally budgeted at $11 billion, but ended up costing $26 billion. To be brought back within Gramm-Rudman-Hollings deficit-reduction targets, these farm program expenses would have to be reduced by roughly $24 billion over the next five years. In the midst of this painful domestic farm cost-reduction dilemma, where will the additional budget resources be found to finance an escalating export subsidy war?

A fourth and final disadvantage to be considered is the greater vulnerability of U.S. agricultural exporters to competitive bilateral *import* restrictions. It would not take long for an escalating export subsidy contest, in third-country markets, to spill over into a competitive race to close off borders to protect *home* markets from foreign farm imports. As a large exporter, the United States would once again enter such a competition at a strategic disadvantage since it would have more existing bilateral sales with its trade rivals placed at risk.

In 1985, for example, the United States sold $5.3 billion in farm goods directly to the EC, while purchasing only $3.4 billion of EC farm products in return. So if a farm trade war between the United States and the EC were to spread into the arena of competitive import restrictions, America would have roughly 50 percent more of its bilateral farm trade vulnerable to interruption. Until now, the EC has felt obliged, under the rules and procedures of GATT, to leave at least part of its large internal market open to U.S. farm goods. The "zero-duty binding" on products such as soybeans and corn gluten feed, pledged during the Dillon Round, has yet to be conspicuously breached. In the context of an escalating farm trade war with the United States, this habit of restraint would become more difficult for the EC to maintain.[15]

Put all of these relative disadvantages together, and it is no wonder that the United States, until now, has stopped short of launching an all-out agricultural trade war. The careful efforts made to estimate the commercial and budgetary cost of such a war have all been profoundly discouraging.

The Costs of an Export Subsidy Competition

Most farm trade war scenarios begin with an escalating export subsidy competition, most often in international grain markets, and usually between the United States and the EC. According to the orthodoxy of neoclassical economics, such a competition will invariably be "irrational" because both subsidizing exporters will always suffer a net welfare loss. Only the importers will gain. This orthodoxy is undoubtedly correct when the alternative is perfectly efficient free trade. In fairness, however, the rationality of export subsidies must today be measured against the alternative of an already costly set of surplus-generating domestic farm programs. From this unfortunate starting point, under some circumstances the subsequent use of export subsidies to dispose of the resulting surplus abroad could in fact become rational, at least from a policymaker's perspective.[16] For the United States, the attraction of using export subsidies would depend on at least three things: the cost and content of existing U.S. domestic farm programs; the elasticity of foreign demand (how much more will the world market buy, especially from the United States, if subsidies are used to lower the U.S. export price); and, competitor response (whether competitors will offset the U.S. export subsidy with larger subsidies of their own).

It is possible to imagine some circumstances in which at least the first two of these requirements might be met. Some U.S. farm programs have been so wasteful (for example, the 1983 PIK acreage-reduction program) that the alternative of spending more on export subsidies might have accomplished just as much at a lower cost. And in some foreign farm markets (for example, in poor countries where low foreign exchange earnings can be a serious bottleneck to larger farm imports) the use of subsidies to lower U.S. export prices might indeed lead to a more than proportionate increase in total foreign sales, including more U.S. sales.

The third requirement, however, is unlikely to be met. When the United States begins spending more on export subsidies, other exporters usually find it affordable enough to do the same, to protect their markets. If they do, most gains to U.S. agriculture will be negated. In international grain markets, it may take the response of only one large rival exporter, such as the EC, to nullify most export subsidy gains to the United States. Market studies which have been built around an assumption of EC counter-subsidies make this abundantly clear. One such study uses a small model of international wheat markets to simulate what might have happened if the United States had decided in 1983 to offer an across-the-board $34-per-ton subsidy on all of its wheat exports (instead of implementing the PIK acreage-reduction program) to reduce U.S. surplus stocks.[17] This simulation realistically assumes that the EC will counter-subsidize as much as necessary to preserve its existing *volume* of foreign wheat sales.

The simulation indicates that a $34-per-ton U.S. subsidy might have been enough to induce the rest of the world to absorb an additional 300 million bushels of U.S. wheat during the 1983/84 marketing year, resulting in roughly a 20 percent increase in U.S. export volume. The direct budget cost of such a subsidy, however, would have been considerable, totalling nearly $1.6 billion, or roughly $5.30 for each of the *additional* 300 million bushels exported. In considering only these budget costs and benefits, it is clear that the United States could have disposed of 300 million bushels of wheat less expensively by simply purchasing that quantity at the $3.65 loan rate and then destroying it. U.S. wheat producers would have experienced no immediate price loss or gain in either case, since the remaining total supply of U.S. wheat would have remained large enough to keep domestic farm prices equivalent to the loan rate.

The international impact of this hypothetical 1983 U.S. wheat export subsidy program is also revealing. A part of the U.S. export gain realized in this case would have come from an enlarged total market, not just from reduced sales by foreign competitors. Some decrease in sales would be suffered by those assumed not to be offering counter-subsidies, such as Canada, Australia, and Argentina. The study indicates, however, that the EC would be able to avoid losing any of its existing volume of foreign wheat sales by increasing its spending on wheat export restitutions by only a small amount, just $400 million. This would be only one-quarter of the budget funds spent by the United States to launch the subsidy initiative in the first place.

It is also true that in this hypothetical case, the EC would have to take a loss in foreign exchange earnings if it decided to use offsetting export subsidies to hold on to its existing volume of exports. The United States, however, would suffer a significant foreign exchange loss as well, since every ton of wheat leaving American shores would be earning $34 less. The somewhat larger volume of total U.S. sales achieved by this subsidy would not be enough in the short run to offset this much smaller per-unit foreign sales value.

The only real winners in this simulation were the importing countries, the biggest of which gained the most. The Soviet Union alone, in 1983/84, would have saved roughly $700 million under this hypothetical U.S. subsidy initiative. The implications seem clear enough: an across-the-board subsidy on U.S. wheat exports would provide windfall gains to importers such as the Soviet Union while producing only a small increase in the volume of U.S. wheat exports, no decrease in the volume of EC wheat exports, a loss of U.S. foreign exchange earnings, and a much heavier budget burden for the United States than for the EC.

Upon considering these problems associated with across-the-board export subsidies, some enthusiasts have advocated using only "targeted" export subsidies, which would concentrate the incentive to "buy American" only in those markets where others were already using subsidies, or only in those markets most responsive to price inducements. The advantage of this approach is that it avoids an expensive price depreciation of all U.S. farm exports. The risk is that it leaves some foreign markets uncovered by subsidies, and hence vulnerable to an equally targeted competitor response. If the United States decides to offer only a targeted export subsidy, in one foreign market but not in another, the competitor that was previously selling in that market can move its own subsidy offer to the untargeted market and preserve its market share at no added cost. For this reason, targeted export subsidies tend to produce dramatic trade shifts, but few aggregate trade gains.

In simulations which assume that competitors will *not* respond to targeted U.S. subsidies with counter-targeted subsidies of their own, affordable gains can be promised for U.S. agriculture.[18] In studies with more realistic assumptions, however, competitor response nullifies most of the expected advantage. This was the case in a 1986 study of targeted export subsidies prepared inside the U.S. Department of Agriculture, which simulated the results of a targeted export subsidy initiative by the United States for wheat and coarse grain, assuming that the EC would respond by increasing its export-restitution payments as much as necessary to retain its existing volume of foreign sales. It also postulated that the United States would cap its targeted subsidies the moment the budget cost exceeded the value to U.S. agriculture of the additional foreign sales being made. The finding was that a targeted U.S. export subsidy program of this kind, if it had been undertaken in 1980, would have increased U.S. wheat exports by only 3 percent, from 36 million tons up to just 37 million tons.[19] The results for coarse grains, due to price elasticity differences, were more encouraging. Even these conclusions were probably on the optimistic side, however, because they were based on "perfect knowledge" regarding which markets would respond to targeted subsidies and which would not, and because several other exporting nations— not just the EC—might also choose to respond with targeted counter-subsidies. The authors also hint at the danger of an escalating trade war that might include competitor retaliations against U.S. farm products on the import side.

Export Subsidy Competition in Practice

In estimating the costs and benefits of an export subsidy competition we do not have to rely entirely upon hypothetical examples. We can examine actual results from an export subsidy initiative recently undertaken by the United States, the so-called Export-Enhancement Program (EEP), which was formally initiated in 1985 and is still underway at this writing.

Export subsidies have historically played only a modest role in the expansion of American farm sales abroad. When U.S. farm exports were expanding most rapidly during the mid-1970s, export subsidies had actually been suspended, and were therefore not a factor at all. Only when foreign sales began to decline seriously, after 1981, did the costly expedient of using export subsidies begin to re-gain some political attraction. The origins of the current Export-Enhancement Program can be traced to January 1983, when the United States decided to provide 1 million tons of wheat flour to Egypt (roughly two-thirds of Egypt's annual needs) under a heavy subsidy that allowed this U.S. flour to undercut subsidized EC offerings by roughly $10–$25 per ton. The United States decided to take this action as a retaliation against EC wheat flour subsidies when it became clear that dispute-settlement procedures under the new GATT Subsidies Code were going to provide no satisfaction.

The results of the initiative were mixed at best. Under the original terms of the sale agreement, Egypt promised not to import wheat flour on a commercial basis from any non-U.S. supplier until June 1984, a promise which was extracted to prevent the EC from buying back the Egyptian market with still larger counter-subsidies. The short-run consequence was a successful displacement of French wheat flour sales from the Egyptian market and a momentary takeover of that market by the United States.

EC exporters were angered by this U.S. subsidy initiative, but only momentarily set back. Temporarily unable to market wheat flour in Egypt, the EC stepped up its subsidized exports of *unmilled* wheat, announcing a 320,000-ton sale to Egypt in early spring. New subsidized EC wheat sales were also made to Iran, Syria, Libya, and Algeria. Within only a few months the EC also announced a surprising 600,000-ton wheat sale to China, a favorite U.S. market which the Community had previously been willing to leave alone. To make this 1983 sale to China, the EC added a special $6-per-ton freight subsidy to its regular $76-per-ton export-restitution payment. The EC also began competing more aggressively with the United States for wheat sales in Latin American markets, where too it had shown little previous interest.

France was particularly determined to stand up to the U.S. wheat flour challenge and began lobbying aggressively within the EC for direct counter-retaliation, including on the import side against U.S. soybeans and corn gluten feed. In August 1983 the EC Commission recommended going forward with more restrictions on both of these imported U.S. products. Then in October, despite a momentarily acute EC farm budget crisis (severe enough to force a temporary suspension of all internal farm subsidy payments), the Community decided to increase its own wheat flour export restitutions by 10 percent. This was enough to win a new agreement with Egypt itself for 500,000 tons of future sales.

At this point, late in 1983, the United States decided to pull back from an escalating wheat flour war with the Community.

The total direct cost of subsidizing the original 1-million-ton U.S. sale had been roughly $180 million (including a $30-per-ton freight differential on the share of this flour that had to be shipped in more expensive U.S. bottoms). The export subsidy had been provided not in cash but "in kind" through gifts to U.S. millers of surplus wheat out of government stocks. Even assuming some reduction in Commodity Credit Corporation (CCC) reserve storage payments, the financial cost to the United States of arranging this unconvincing and ineffective retaliation against the EC had outweighed the benefit.

Despite this disappointing experience, two years later in June 1985 Congress was again insisting that some form of subsidy be used to reverse the continuing decline of U.S. farm exports. In part to block an even more extreme congressional subsidy initiative, the administration replied by initiating the Export-Enhancement Program. Modeled after the earlier Egyptian wheat flour sale, it was also an "in kind" export subsidy program, with the CCC making cheap foreign sales possible by giving free "bonus bushels" out of surplus stocks to U.S. exporters. With congressional support, this new "export PIK" program was written formally into the 1985 farm bill with a mandate to dispense $2 billion of surplus government commodities to U.S. exporters, so as to lower the price of American sales in those markets where the United States was at a disadvantage due to large EC export-restitution payments.

While it is still too early to judge the final success of EEP, several disturbing problems have already become visible. First, the EEP has shown a tendency to produce large additional U.S. sales in some individual markets, but little increase in U.S. sales overall. Shipments of U.S. wheat and wheat products went up sharply to markets in North Africa and the Middle East, where most early EEP sales were concentrated beginning in late 1985. Total U.S. sales in these markets during the first fiscal year the program was in effect (October 1985/September 1986) increased by 73 percent, and EC sales to these targeted markets momentarily declined.[20] Total U.S. wheat exports *to all markets*, however, did not increase during this period. Before the implementation of EEP, during the July 1984/June 1985 year, U.S. wheat and flour exports to all markets totalled 38.1 million tons. Under

EEP, during the 1985/86 year, this export total actually *fell* to just 25 million tons, a decline of roughly one-third. The U.S. share of world wheat and wheat flour markets also fell from 37 percent to 29 percent, while the EC share increased slightly from 17.3 percent to 18.2 percent.[21] EEP export subsidies in 1986 were altering the direction of some U.S. farm trade, but without doing much to reverse the declining volume of that trade. The United States managed temporarily to displace some EC exports to markets in North Africa and the Middle East, but those exports only went into other uncovered markets—such as Brazil, China, and the Soviet Union—where U.S. sales were displaced.

Another predictable disappointment has been an EC willingness to match EEP subsidy expenditures even in some contested markets with larger export restitutions. In September 1986, for example, the EC challenged EEP directly by increasing its own export subsidy offerings by $11 per ton on grain and flour sales to Algeria, Morocco, Egypt, and Syria. Thanks to this increase, a sale of 200,000 tons of French wheat was made to Algeria. Then a few days later—and for one day only—the EC raised its wheat export restitutions for Algeria by another $18 dollars per ton, and 277,800 more tons of wheat were sold. Earlier, in June 1986, the EC had also raised restitution payments for barley sales to Saudi Arabia, Algeria, Israel, and Jordan. As a result, these nations, which had all been targets for EEP barley sales, made 210,000 tons of new purchases from the EC.[22]

A third disturbing aspect of the EEP has been its tendency to spark political and diplomatic controversy. The EEP was originally designed to exclude sales to the Soviet Union, which would otherwise have become the program's single largest subsidy recipient.[23] Unfortunately, this exclusion gave the Soviet Union a convenient excuse to back out of its long-term commitment under a 1983 agreement to purchase a minimum of 4 million tons of U.S. wheat each year. The Soviet Union decided to fall short of this minimum by 1.1 million tons in 1985, claiming that it had no obligation to import at a higher price than other U.S. customers. During the first nine months of the 1986 agreement year, the Soviets then made almost no wheat purchases at all from the United States (only 0.15 million tons) and continued to complain about their exclusion from the EEP. Under pressure from domestic producers and exporters, the U.S. government finally reversed itself and announced that the Soviet Union would be eligible for EEP bonus bushels, at least for the limited purpose of meeting its 4-million-ton minimum import commitment.

This initial extension of the EEP to include the Soviet Union embarrassed U.S. diplomacy, antagonized U.S. farm export competitors, and did not lead immediately to any additional Soviet purchases of U.S. wheat. Secretary of State George Shultz, who had opposed the decision, commented publicly that the Soviets must be "chortling and scratching their heads about a system that says we're going to fix it up so that the American taxpayers make it possible for a Soviet housewife to buy American-produced food at prices lower than an American housewife."[24] Stiff protests came from Canadian Prime Minister Brian Mulroney and from Australian Prime Minister Robert Hawke. In Canberra, a delegation of Australian farmers marched from Parliament House to the U.S. Embassy, dumped wheat on the lawn, and presented the U.S. Ambassador with letters of protest. These angry reactions, on the eve of the Punta del Este GATT Ministerial meeting, had the unfortunate effect of drawing criticism away from the far more extensive and objectionable export subsidy programs of the EC. The 1986 decision to offer EEP subsidies to the Soviet Union was also a failure on its own terms, since Moscow decided for the moment to ignore the U.S. subsidy offer. The reasons were largely financial. Instead of purchasing U.S. wheat subsidized at $15 per ton, the Soviet Union bought 1 million tons of French wheat, which was made cheaper because it was more generously subsidized at $125 per ton.

A final problem with the EEP has been the difficulty of expanding its size at an affordable cost. The administration of the program, which for each sale involves a complicated multistage bid system, has been a serious impediment to growth. Other things as well make the expanded use of an "in kind" export subsidy program inherently difficult. PIK subsidy programs are superficially more attractive for budget-accounting purposes than cash programs, because they use existing government stocks rather than cash to pay exporters. The larger these PIK subsidy programs become, however, the more they risk depressing the market by moving previously isolated government stocks into free supply. The resulting downward pressure on domestic market prices is not only unwelcome to U.S. farm producers; it can also backfire on budget officials by pushing more new crop production into government commodity loan programs, costing money and adding to government stocks in a "revolving door" fashion.

In anticipation of some of these inherent problems, the EEP was cut in size in March 1986, just three months after it was formally enacted into law. At that point only about $120 million of U.S. surplus commodities had actually been disposed of through completed EEP sales, and, because the program was moving so slowly, its funding base quickly became vulnerable to competing demands. In order to find the budgetary room necessary to pay for some other costly changes in domestic farm programs, Congress itself decided to cut mandated/authorized EEP funding in half, to only $1 billion/$1.5 billion over three years.[25]

Soon thereafter, however, the program began to expand once again. Bonus bushel offers were made not only to the Soviet Union, but also to Poland and China, and all eventually responded with purchases. Early in 1987 the Soviet Union finally agreed to 4 million tons of wheat purchases, thanks to more generous subsidy offers of more than $40 per ton. When it appeared that the EEP authorized budget ceiling was soon to be broken because of such large subsidies, Congress changed cost-accounting procedures inside USDA so as to allow bonus bushel sales to continue, and initiated legislation to broaden the market area covered and to expand the EEP budget back up above the $2 billion range. The EC, meanwhile, continued to match the United States subsidy-for-subsidy. In March 1987 it even expanded the competition decisively, with subsidized sales of 750,000 tons of corn to ten separate importing countries in North Africa, the Middle East and Eastern Europe. This EC move into corn subsidies inspired the U.S. Feed Grains Council to urge a retaliatory expansion of the EEP to include corn as well.

Those who had hoped that the beginning of the Uruguay Round of GATT talks would help to contain this unfortunate U.S.-EC export subsidy competition have therefore been disappointed.[26] In fact, the tactical need to create "bargaining chips" for those talks has given subsidy enthusiasts in the U.S. farm community just one more excuse to ask for EEP expansion. By March 1987 even U.S. Trade Representative Clayton Yeutter had been pressured by these groups into endorsing a further expansion of the EEP as a "tactical tool" to bring reluctant trade partners to the negotiating table.

Alternatives to an Export Subsidy War

This difficult and disappointing experience with export subsidies need not lead to a conclusion that all U.S. agricultural export promotion policies are unaffordable or counterproductive. A variety of such policies can provide useful support to U.S. agriculture without bringing on excessive budget costs, imperiling the GATT talks, or provoking competitor retaliation. Least provocative of all are well-established U.S. "food for peace" (PL 480) food aid programs, continuously in use since 1954. PL 480 Title II programs (authorized at $762 million in the 1986 fiscal year) make an absolutely vital contribution to famine relief in poor countries. PL 480 Title I/III programs (authorized at $902 million) are an essential component of U.S. diplomatic and assistance policy, especially in the politically volatile Middle East. The multipurpose nature of these food aid programs, in combination with their generally modest and predictable size, has thus far discouraged retaliation by export competitors.

Export credit guarantee programs (such as the CCC GSM-102 program, recently authorized at $4.8 billion) are also more affordable, while playing a less provocative role in supporting the growth of U.S. farm exports. Export credit guarantees help heavily indebted importing countries to arrange the bank financing necessary to continue purchasing U.S. farm products. This has become a much needed form of assistance, especially in Latin American countries such as Mexico and Chile, where large external debts have left the U.S. market position highly credit-sensitive. If properly managed, export credit guarantees do not have to result in unacceptable budget outlays. In recent years, in fact, U.S. export credit guarantee programs have not even been used up to their authorized potential. Due to slow allocations and inadequate reallocations, only about one-half of the funding recently authorized for GSM-102 has actually been put to use. An even less well-utilized program is GSM-103, an intermediate-term credit program designed to further market development by helping to finance projects in importing countries which might facilitate farm purchases from the United States, such as port development, handling and distribution structures, processing plants, and livestock and herd improvement efforts. GSM-103 has been on the books for eight years, but no projects have been approved and no funds recently authorized.[27]

In early 1987, as part of its larger effort to trim the farm budget, the Reagan Administration proposed a $2 billion reduction in export credit guarantees. The justification for this action was the underutilization of past loan authority. But this had been due in large part to noncompetitive U.S. farm export prices caused by high domestic commodity loan rates and high dollar exchange rates.[28] Given that commodity loan rates and dollar exchange rates have declined since 1986, making U.S. commodity export prices competitive once again, and since the Latin American debt crisis continues largely unabated, this may not be time to cut back so sharply on export credit guarantee authority.

When considering these various alternatives to launching a costly and self-defeating export subsidy war, the United States need not feel that it is giving up all of its options to get "tough" with foreign trade competitors. Aggressive actions—including threats of direct retaliation—are at times necessary to dissuade foreign trade rivals from ignoring their well-established agricultural trade obligations. In circumstances where trade obligations are not well-established, however, "tough" talk is unlikely to be effective. Trade rivals will probably decide to call the bluff, knowing as they do that in any full-scale farm trade war the export-dependent U.S. farm sector is still positioned to lose the most. In contrast, it is where trade obligations are well-established in the rules of GATT that U.S. threats to undertake discrete retaliations against rule violations become more contained and credible. A willingness to make such threats, and if necessary to carry them out, is an essential element of U.S. farm trade diplomacy.

To illustrate this point, consider two instances when the United States was able to deter blatant violations of GATT rules by the EC. First, in 1983, the United States used credible threats of retaliation to turn back an EC Commission proposal to limit the import of nongrain feeds, and to tax nondairy fats and oils. Either step, if taken without adequate compensation to the United States, would have been a clear infringement of GATT obligations. Knowing that they had GATT rules on their side, U.S. officials responded promptly and firmly, personally delivering formal protests to the EC Commission and to all member-country governments. More pointedly, the U.S. Secretary of Agriculture sent a letter directly to the EC Agriculture Commissioner, explaining the likelihood of retaliation. The Undersecretary of Agriculture was sent on a tour of European capitals for face-to-face talks on the dispute, and the U.S. Treasury Secretary simultaneously sent a letter of protest to all European finance ministers. To climax this effective effort at signaling U.S. concern, representatives of all EC member states were called to the State Department in Washington for further lecturing on the subject. Although the French representative declined to attend this meeting, noone could question the likelihood of U.S. retaliation if the EC went forward with its plans. The subsequent EC Council decision against imposing the recommended tax on nondairy fats and oils and to move slowly on proposals for a cap on corn gluten feed imports was clearly influenced by these well-timed U.S. threats and objections.

A second instance in which the United States was able to use threats of retaliation with some success was in a GATT compensation dispute with the EC following the 1986 Community enlargement. Had the United States not been willing to threaten retaliation in this case, a loss of more than $400 million of farm sales to Spain might have gone uncompensated. Since the EC obligation to provide compensation was an unambiguous rule in GATT, U.S. threats to secure the compensation, through unilateral import restrictions if necessary, became a credible, contained, and effective response. In December 1986, after months of no progress, higher U.S. tariffs on $400 million of EC food and beverage sales to the United States were tentatively announced to set a one month deadline for EC concessions. The EC offers that were subsequently made fell far short of full compensation, but they were large enough to permit a face-saving resolution of the dispute.[29] If it had not been honorably resolved, U.S. farm lobby resentments would have intensified, and a mutually damaging farm trade war between the United States and the EC would have immediately become more likely.

Threats of retaliation against the EC remain, by themselves, a fragile basis on which to pursue U.S. external agricultural trade interests. This was illustrated not long after the resolution of the 1986 enlargement dispute, when French corn growers managed to take back some of the "compensation" that had been given to the United States in Spain and Portugal by securing export subsidies (as previously mentioned) for their own corn sales to U.S. markets in North Africa and the Middle East. In February 1987 the EC Commission also revived its earlier proposal for an internal consumption tax on nondairy fats and oils, in part to help fund its expensive internal oilseed production subsidies. This put U.S. soybean sales at risk. Formal threats of U.S. retaliation were again issued, not unlike those made successfully in 1983. Unfortunately, this time around, Community resentment toward American "trade war" tactics had intensified, along with the internal budget pressures which had created their need for the tax. In this instance, it was uncertain whether there would be such a restrained EC response.

Conclusion

We have seen that the international farm trade policy alternatives available to the United States outside of GATT are fraught with risks and dangers. The option of trying to "manage" farm trade outside of GATT by negotiating illiberal international commodity agreements is especially unattractive to the United States, given the tendency of such agreements either to work to the relative disadvantage of low-cost U.S. farm producers, or to be broken by less disciplined foreign trade rivals. Equally unattractive is the option of trying to "coerce" foreign trade rivals into giving up market shares through threats of launching a general farm trade war. The United States is not well-positioned, for both strategic and tactical reasons, to prevail in an export subsidy competition, and it would be more vulnerable than any other major trader if that competition spilled over into a war of bilateral import restrictions. If U.S. threats to launch a general farm trade war ever had to be carried out, and if foreign trade rivals retaliated in kind, U.S. agriculture would stand to lose the most.

There is room outside of GATT for the use of some less provocative instruments of U.S. farm export promotion, ranging from food aid to export credit guarantees. There are even times for making "tough" threats of direct, but contained, retaliation against rivals who contemplate ignoring their well-established farm trade obligations. Yet the basis for these trade obligations remains, more often than not, the GATT itself.

The success of GATT does require that important parallel policy initiatives be taken outside of its framework. As we shall see, however, most of these supporting steps must be taken in the domestic, rather than the international, arena. The difficult task of fixing farm trade abroad requires, in the first instance, a determined effort by the major trading nations to repair farm policy at home. U.S. leadership in this domestic farm policy reform process is in fact the key to securing comprehensive reforms in the international arena.

Notes

1. For a closer look at a number of past and current ICAs in other product markets, see World Bank, *World Development Report 1986, op. cit.*, Chapter 7.

2. See Geoff Miller, *The Political Economy of International Agricultural Policy Reform, op. cit.*, p. 117.

3. The reference wheat was No. 1 Manitoba Northern. Prices of other wheats were not set specifically, but price differentials were watched by an Advisory Committee on Price Equivalents, and the disputes that occurred were dealt with by the Executive Committee of the intergovernmental International Wheat Council (IWC) in London.

4. Jon McLin, "Surrogate International Organization and the Case of World Food Security, 1949–69," *International Organization*, vol. 33, no. 1 (Winter 1979), pp. 35–54.

5. With U.S.-EC farm trade differences never very far below the surface, most of the negotiating time that went into this effort was spent trying to resolve a disagreement between the United States and the EC on whether quantity-triggered or price-triggered rules should be used to define each nation's grain reserve management obligations. Late in 1978 the United States finally accepted the EC position that price triggers should govern the release and acquisition of stocks. By then, however, the United States was already rebuilding its own stocks unilaterally, as its domestic farm programs began to dictate, once prices fell. Due to lower prices and growing U.S. stocks, the sense of urgency passed. The less developed importing countries in particular became less interested in joining an international arrangement when their side demands for more economic aid were not met.

6. Economic Policy Council of UNA-USA, "A U.S. Initiative Toward World Food Security," Report of the Grains Policy Panel, United Nations Association of the USA, New York, October 1980, p. 8.

7. Dale E. Hathaway, Testimony before the House of Representatives Committee on Agriculture, Hearings on World Hunger, July 22, 1981.

8. *Cargill Bulletin*, (May 1984), p. 5.

9. U.S. Department of Agriculture, Foreign Agriculture Circular, FG-10-86 (August 1986) and FG-7-85 (May 1985).

10. Statement by Carroll G. Brunthaver before Senate Agricultural Subcommittee on Foreign Agricultural Policy, July 29, 1986.

11. It is not only in grain markets that the EC has been unable, thus far, to restrain its own production and trade. In international dairy markets it was an EC decision, late in 1984, to sell 223 kt of old butter to the Soviet Union that breached the terms of the 1979 International Dairy Arrangement, which had originally been agreed to in the course of the Tokyo Round of GATT negotiations.

12. See "U.S. Agriculture Still Has the Edge," *Farmline*, vol. 6, no. 10 (November 1985), p. 9.

13. Comparing U.S. and foreign production costs is made difficult by such things as fluctuating land prices and currency exchange rates. There is one USDA study of comparative *variable* costs of production (not including labor, land, and depreciation) using data from 1980–82 (before the strongest surge in dollar exchange rates) which showed U.S. farms in a strong competitive position not only

against the EC, but even against some of the lowest-cost foreign competitors in Australia, Canada, and the developing world. Average variable costs per bushel for U.S. wheat on the Northern Plains were almost identical to Canadian costs in Saskatchewan, and U.S. national average costs were below Australian national average costs. Average U.S. variable costs for soybeans in the cornbelt were well below variable costs in both Argentina and Brazil. For corn, the U.S. variable cost advantage is extremely strong throughout the Northern Hemisphere. Argentina can produce corn more cheaply, but high internal transportation costs nullify most of this advantage. See "U.S. Agriculture Still Has the Edge," *Farmline*, vol. 6, no. 10 (November 1985), pp. 8–9.

14. The National Commission on Agricultural Trade and Export Policy, which presented its findings in 1986, listed as its first recommendation that the United States take "aggressive action to meet and counteract the effects of unfair foreign trade practices." At the same time, the Commission recommends that GATT be used to negotiate the "elimination or substantial reduction of constraints to fair and open trade." See "Concluding Recommendations of the National Commission on Agricultural Trade and Export Policy: Executive Summary of the Report to the President and Congress of the United States of America," Washington, 1986.

15. Duty-free U.S. soybean sales to the EC (nearly one-half of all U.S. soybean exports) would be a particularly inviting target for bilateral import retaliation. The Community could either impose a mix of levies and quotas at the border, and then refuse to offer adequate compensation under GATT, or it could introduce an internal tax on the consumption of nondairy fats and oils, and then try to argue that such a tax is GATT-legal. Such a consumption tax (proposed by the EC Commission in 1983, and again in 1987) would be a very tempting step for the Community, since it could earn as much as 2 billion ECU in revenue for the EC budget, finance EC oilseed subsidies, and increase the consumption of surplus EC products at the same time that it was damaging U.S. soybean sale prospects. The EC has refrained from imposing such a tax until now both because of its GATT obligations and internal objections from its own oilseed-crushing industry. These considerations might be swept aside in the context of an open-ended farm trade war with the United States.

16. Philip L. Paarlberg, "When Are Export Subsidies Rational?" *Agricultural Economics Research*, vol. 36, no. 1 (Winter 1984), pp. 1–7.

17. Jerry Sharples, "Are Export Subsidies the Answer to U.S. Grain Surpluses?" (Staff Paper No. 84-10, International Economics Division, Economic Research Service, U.S. Department of Agriculture in Cooperation with Department of Agricultural Economics, Purdue University, October 1984).

18. See, for example, "The Economic Benefit of Increasing U.S. Wheat Exports" (A study prepared for the National Association of Wheat Growers and U.S. Wheat Associates, October 31, 1984). This study proposes targeting twenty individual nonindustrial wheat importing countries with expanded use of PL 480 Titles I and II food aid, GSM-102 commercial-credit guarantees, credit guarantees blended with interest-free GSM-5 credits, GSM-301 intermediate-term credits, and an export PIK program. It estimates that the United States might, as a consequence, be able to increase its wheat exports, within five years, by about 180 million bushels, or 5 million tons, at a total cost of only $90 million in actual budget outlays, or only $0.50 per bushel of additional wheat exports. All of these estimates, however, require an assumption that competitors such as the EC will respond not with counter-subsidies, but with production and export reductions instead.

19. U.S. Department of Agriculture, Economic Research Service, "Embargoes, Surplus Disposal, and U.S. Agriculture: A Summary," U.S. Department of Agriculture, *Agriculture Information Bulletin,* no. 503 (November 1986), p. 32.

20. U.S. Department of Agriculture, Foreign Agriculture Circular, Grains, FG-12-86 (October 1986), p. 7.

21. U.S. Department of Agriculture, Foreign Agriculture Circular, Grains, FG-14-86 (December 1986), p. 9.

22. "Farm Exports à la Carte: How Europe's System Works," *Journal of Commerce,* October 3, 1986, p. 16B.

23. Also excluded in the original design of the program were nations such as Poland, Saudi Arabia, China, and Iraq. All were later made eligible for EEP subsidies. In November 1986 Syria was barred from further eligibility.

24. "U.S.S.R. Shuns Wheat Deal," *Journal of Commerce,* September 5, 1986, p. 16B.

25. Congress also decided in 1986 to cut another subsidy program, the Targeted Export Assistance (TEA) program, by more than half to only $110 million annually. The TEA program uses surplus CCC stocks to reimburse agricultural organizations for all or part of the authorized export promotion programs they undertake. TEA was

originally designed to boost sales of U.S. commodities that had received favorable rulings in Section 301 trade complaints, but had yet to gain compensation. These commodities included frozen potatoes, canned fruit, raisins, citrus, walnuts, and wood products. Some 80 percent of the actual $110 million of TEA allocations in fiscal 1986 went to support high-value and processed farm exports.

26. In March 1987, the chairman of the Australian Wheat Board accused the United States and the EC of being "hell-bent on destroying the international wheat market" with export subsidies, and of refusing to discuss solutions in GATT.

27. *Cargill Bulletin*, (October 1986), p. 2.

28. When U.S. export prices are not competitive, extending export credit guarantees can actually backfire. In 1982, when the United States extended $1.3 billion in GSM-102 to Mexico, one result was a momentary surplus in the Mexican foreign exchange account, which allowed Mexico to make a part of its 1983 farm import purchases for cash, from lower-cost (non-U.S.) sources.

29. The EC agreed to offer a 2.3-million-ton quota for all imports of corn and sorghum into Spain under a reduced levy until December 31, 1990. The United States could expect to sell about 75 percent of this tonnage. The EC also dropped a 15.5 percent market reserve for EC grains in Portugal, which could lead to an additional 350,000 tons of Portuguese grain imports. The EC also agreed to the permanent duty-free entry of U.S. soybeans and corn gluten feed into Spain and Portugal, but any sales of corn gluten feed would be deducted from the grain quota. The U.S. Feed Grains Council denounced the agreement as "totally unsatisfactory," and it did fall short of compensating U.S. agriculture for all of the $400–$600 million in farm trade being lost in Spain, particularly. But the 2.3-million-ton reduced levy quota finally offered by the EC in late January 1987, following threatened U.S. retaliation, was at least an improvement over the 1.6-million-ton quota offered previously.

Four

How to Fix Farm Trade: Domestic Farm Policy Reform

When looking for ways to fix farm trade, we cannot afford to spend all of our time chasing after the detrimental actions of foreign governments abroad. In international agricultural markets the United States can sometimes exercise greater influence simply by adjusting its own domestic food and farm programs at home. Since the United States is by far the largest and still the world's most efficient producer of so many tradable farm products, its domestic farm policies can by themselves determine much of the structure and condition of international agricultural trade. This being the case, what changes might be taken in U.S. domestic food and farm policy to improve the performance of U.S. international agricultural trade? To answer this question we must examine the substance of the current domestic farm legislation passed by Congress in the 1985 farm bill. We will then be in a position to review both the domestic and farm trade implications of several recently proposed alternatives to current legislation.

The 1985 Farm Bill

When Congress began to debate the reauthorization of U.S. domestic farm legislation in early 1985, U.S. farm exports were in the fourth year of a sharp and disastrous decline. It was widely recognized that this deterioration had been brought on, at least in part, by the high support prices—especially for grains—which had been written into the previous farm bill enacted in 1981. High domestic support prices had been written into that earlier law under a mistaken assumption that high rates of inflation would probably continue in the U.S. economy during the first half of the 1980s. When tight U.S. monetary policies first cut down inflation, and then threw the world economy into a recession in 1982, these high and inflexible domestic support prices led to serious domestic supply and international trade imbalances.

High and inflexible domestic price-support guarantees after 1981 gave U.S. farmers the choice of producing for their own government at home rather than in a more realistic response to demand abroad. When foreign demand began to lag in 1982, U.S. farmers began exercising this option. U.S. exports fell, but U.S. production continued to expand. Farmers who could not receive a high price in the market, sold instead to their government by defaulting on commodity loans. Government-owned surplus stocks, as a consequence, began to grow unacceptably large. In order to reduce the surpluses, which are expensive to carry, the government decided in 1983, under the PIK program, to induce U.S. farmers to take large portions of their cropland out of production. Foreign competitors were pleased to see U.S. policy propping up world prices in this fashion, and seized the opportunity to expand their own production accordingly. Foreign farm exports therefore continued to expand, and U.S. farm exports continued to decline.

Going into the 1985 farm bill debate, the primary objective of the administration was to remedy this self-defeating situation by reducing domestic farm price supports—both loan rates and target prices. Unfortunately, the legislation that was finally passed lowered loan rates dramatically, but left high target prices essentially unchanged. The result has been the emergence of an even more serious domestic farm budget imbalance. The severity of the situation has triggered a search for affordable alternatives to the 1985 farm bill. The ultimate choice between these alternatives will have large implications for farm trade.

It is essential to understand that the U.S. government uses two separate price policy instruments to support farmers—commodity loan rates, and target prices. Loan rates tend to determine the price that foreign customers and domestic consumers will pay for U.S. farm products. Target prices tend to determine how much U.S. farmers will plant each year, and how much the government will spend on farm income-support programs.

Loan rates represent a standing offer by the government (by the CCC) to purchase surplus commodities from farmers at a preset price per bushel, referred to as a "loan rate."[1] Whenever free market prices decline to the level of the loan rate, farmers will start selling (defaulting on their loans) to the CCC. The loan rate thus tends to set a firm floor under free market prices. Basic loan rates are set by law, and operative loan rates are announced for each commodity by the Secretary of Agriculture before the beginning of each marketing year.

Target prices, which are set higher than loan rates, are a second instrument of U.S. domestic farm support policy. They are not a price at which the government offers to purchase products from farmers. They are instead a *price standard*, legislated by Congress, used as a basis for calculating the size of direct cash payments ("deficiency payments") made to farmers. Deficiency payments are calculated as the difference between the target price and the loan rate, or as the difference between the target price and the market price, which ever is smaller. In effect, these payments guarantee farmers a minimum return per bushel, whether they are selling to the government or on the free market.[2] Farmers receive deficiency payments according to individual calculations of their "base acreage" and "program yield" per acre.

At the onset of congressional debate on the 1985 farm bill, the administration argued that *both* commodity loan rates and target prices would have to come down. Lower (more "market-oriented") loan rates and target prices were supposed to help to reduce government stocks and cut budget outlays at home, while restoring the competitiveness of U.S. farm exports abroad. Most domestic farm commodity groups shared the administration's concern about the competitiveness of U.S. farm exports, and so they agreed, through their representatives in Congress, to a rather dramatic reduction in loan rates. In wheat markets, for example, the new farm bill reduced basic U.S. loan rates by 9 percent in 1986, and set them in subsequent years according to a moving average of recent market prices (75–85 percent of average market prices over the preceding five years). These lower basic loan rates could then be reduced even more dramatically year-by-year at the discretion of the Secretary of Agriculture—by as much as another 20 percent for wheat and feedgrains—if deemed necessary to keep U.S. products competitively priced abroad.

While conceding to more market-oriented loan rates, most U.S. domestic farm organizations were not yet willing to give up the cash income guarantees provided by high target prices. Therefore, they agreed to let commodity loan rates fall only if "target prices" remained effectively frozen at the existing high level. In the end the 1985 farm bill legislated a very modest schedule of target price reductions, and only in the out years— for feedgrains and wheat it mandated a mere 2 percent reduction in 1988, 3 percent in 1989, and 5 percent in 1990.

The administration knew that high target prices, when paired with falling loan rates, would oblige the government to spend much more on cash deficiency payments. For example, when 1986 wheat target prices remained frozen at $4.38 per bushel, while the loan rate (along with market prices) suddenly fell to $2.40 a bushel, the entire difference—of roughly $2 a bushel— had to be provided as compensation to participating wheat farmers straight out of the federal budget. Nevertheless, administration efforts in 1985 to prevent this target price freeze were unavailing.[3] Knowing that it needed a finished bill by the end of 1985 in order to renew farm program authorizations, and perhaps blindly believing that an immediate farm export gain would accompany lower loan rates, the administration decided to accept what would soon prove to be an expensive compromise.

At the time, few realized just how expensive the 1985 farm bill would turn out to be. Between 1981 and 1985, under the previous farm bill, federal spending on farm price- and income-support programs averaged about $12 billion a year, which was considered too much, since it was almost four times the $3.4 billion annual spending level of the previous five years. The administration kept hoping that the 1985 farm bill would bring these costs down, and its original estimate for farm program outlays in fiscal 1986 was only $11 billion. Actual budget costs during the first year of the new bill turned out to be more than twice as large, an all-time record $25.8 billion. At this writing, projected outlays for fiscal 1987 are just as extravagant, at $23–$28 billion.[4] At a time of scandalous federal budget deficits and unprecedented forced cutbacks in most other domestic social welfare programs, this sudden hemorrhage in additional farm program spending has come under justifiable criticism.

Early criticism of the 1985 farm bill was all the more intense because in the first year after its passage U.S. agricultural exports failed to show any signs of revival. In the summer of 1986, just as the new bill was beginning to come into effect, the administration even experienced the embarrassment of seeing total monthly export values fall below imports, pushing U.S. agricultural trade into a net deficit for the first time in more than twenty-five years. Some of this decline in exports early in 1986 should have been expected, since it took more than six months for the announced lowering of U.S. loan rates to work its way through the crop year to produce lower export prices. Foreign customers suspended their purchases in the meantime, in anticipation of the better deal certain to materialize down the road. Foreign competitors simultaneously offered larger export subsidies in a frantic "last chance" effort to sell all that they could before U.S. prices fell. Expected or not, this perverse short-term trade response in 1986, together with much higher farm budget outlays, badly undermined political support for the recently enacted farm bill, both inside and outside of the administration. In November 1986, Budget Director James Miller announced that he had "grave reservations" about the political survivability of the 1985 farm bill in view of the fact that "It has cost more than we expected and doesn't seem to be effective."

Alternatives to the 1985 Farm Bill

How can the trade and budget shortcomings of the 1985 farm bill be remedied? One obvious way to contain budget costs would be to legislate a reduction of target prices, in line with today's lower loan rates, in order to reduce the size of deficiency payments. A very different alternative would be to reject lower loan rates and turn instead to an inward-looking "domestic supply-management" approach. A third possibility would be to improve both the trade and the market orientation of the 1985 farm bill. This could be achieved by maintaining lower loan rates while "decoupling" cash payments to farmers from production decisions. Let's consider each of these options in turn.

Target Price Reductions

An obvious way to shrink the unacceptable budget exposure in the 1985 farm bill would be to legislate a reduction in target prices. If target prices could be made as "market-oriented" as loan rates, which is what the administration originally intended, then U.S. farm products would retain their new competitive posture in markets abroad, and U.S. farm policy would become more affordable to taxpayers at home.

High target prices have damaged U.S. policy in several ways. In combination with lower loan rates they have first created intolerable budget costs. When the loan rate for wheat fell by $0.90 per bushel in 1986 while the target price remained frozen, implied deficiency payments were increased by more than 80 percent, to nearly $2 per bushel. For corn, implied deficiency payments more than doubled, to $1.11 a bushel.

Second, high target prices stimulate unneeded and inefficient farm production. It is target prices, not loan rates, that determine a farmer's decision to plant. Relatively inefficient U.S. farmers, who should not be planting a crop because their per-bushel production costs are so much greater than market prices (at the new low loan rate), are planting anyway under the 1985 farm bill simply to become eligible for the large cash deficiency payments that high target prices assure them. In 1986, the deficiency payment for wheat was so generous that it added 82.5 percent to the farm value of the loan rate, more than enough to push the anticipated revenue of many inefficient farmers back up to above their high initial production costs. Thus it serves as an incentive for them to remain in production.

Third, while high target prices have been encouraging some *inefficient* farmers to continue planting, they have also been compelling some highly *efficient* farmers to reduce acreage and cut back on production. This is due to the fact that, in recent years, acreage "set-asides" have been required for farmers' deficiency payments. The set-aside requirements tend to increase in lock step with target prices, as a means to offset the stimulus to unneeded production provided by target prices. The Department of Agriculture has estimated that without set-aside and other acreage-reduction programs in 1986, U.S. farmers might have responded to high target price guarantees by planting an additional 25–30 million acres.

Acreage-reduction programs, in the form of either set-asides or separate "paid-diversion" programs (payments can be made in cash or "in kind"), can look like an expedient way to offset some of the production stimulus and some of the budget exposure brought on by high target prices. In reality, they may do little of either. Deficiency payment limitations ($50,000 per farm) reduce the attraction of set-aside program participation for the largest operators—who often happen to be the very farmers whose production should be curtailed. For those who do participate, actual production cutbacks may then be quite small, and many farmers will find a way to set aside only their least productive land, while using deficiency payments to intensify fertilizer and other input use on the good land that they farm. So input distortions will increase, surplus production will continue, and costly government stocks will keep going up, all at the same time.

Fully aware of all these problems generated by high target prices, the administration presented a proposal in 1987 to reduce target prices by 10 percent per year through 1990. It was estimated that reductions on this scale could ease surplus production while saving as much as $13 billion in budget outlays between fiscal 1988 and 1990.[5]

The economic rationale for reducing target prices is unfortunately undercut by obvious political difficulties. The generous deficiency payments being made under the terms of the 1985 farm bill may be unpopular with budget officials, but they are extremely attractive to farmers. Recall that the administration fought the target price reduction battle in Congress in 1985 under relatively favorable political conditions, which included Republican control of the Senate, and they still lost. If this battle were to be refought today—by a lame duck administration facing a Democratic House and Senate, and in the midst of a 1988 presidential election campaign—the result would most likely be the same. The coalition of farm state advocates that preserved high target prices in 1985 would re-organize, partisanship would intrude, and without great fortune—such as a breakthrough in GATT that promised parallel price or production restraints abroad—another loss would be most probable. In February 1987, only one month after taking over as the new Chairman of the Senate Agriculture Committee, Senator Patrick Leahy (D-Vt.) dismissed the administration's proposal to reduce target prices as "unacceptable." Expressing the view of most producer interests, Senator Leahy said, "We're not going to junk our present programs unless we've got a better alternative."[6]

Supply Management

One alternative to the 1985 farm bill which is persistently favored by some "populist" producer interests—especially Great Plains wheat growers—is to boost farm prices and cut farm budget costs simultaneously through tight mandatory controls on farm production. Instead of trying to bring supply into line with demand through a market-oriented adjustment in production incentives, or through competitive export pricing to increase foreign sales, these producers advocate protecting farm income through "supply management" at home.

This approach has several apparent attractions. First, it appears to reduce the dependence of U.S. farm producers on unstable and unreliable foreign markets. Instead of waiting for foreign demand to boost prices, U.S. producers would get what they want by simply agreeing to a coordinated cut in domestic production. Second, supply management appears to promise a reduction in farm budget costs. If an agreement to cut production were made mandatory—following a referendum vote by all producers—then farmers would not have to be "bribed" into making acreage reductions, as is now the case, with expensive deficiency payments. The cost to U.S. consumers of purchasing food and farm products would no doubt increase under this alternative, but since they currently spend a smaller share of their income on food than consumers anywhere else in the world, this might be considered an acceptable price to pay for "saving the family farm."

Champions of the supply-management approach have most recently united behind a so-called "Save the Family Farm Act," sponsored by Senator Tom Harkin (D-Iowa) and Representative Richard Gephardt (D-Mo.). If enacted into law in its most recent form, this legislation would require that producer referendums be held for each commodity (with wheat and feedgrains held jointly) in which a simple majority could approve a program requiring mandatory planting reductions on up to 35 percent of an individual's farm land. To enforce these controls, the government would issue "marketing certificates," determined by acreage base and established yield, which individual farmers would need to present in order to market their commodities. Target prices and deficiency payments would be eliminated, but commodity loan rates would be roughly doubled in order to reach levels equal to 70–80 percent of what farmers still call "parity."[7] Mandatory controls on supply would be expected to boost free market prices enough to make these much higher loan rates affordable to the government.

There are many widely recognized disadvantages to this radical supply-management approach, including, first of all, disadvantages to farmers themselves. High commodity prices brought on by sharp mandatory production cutbacks would help individual field crop farmers in the short run, but many others—including livestock producers who purchase field crops as inputs—would lose. Many farm wage laborers would also suffer because their employment depends upon a high volume of production.

In rural communities which service farm production, the income and employment losses that would accompany mandatory production controls would be even more devastating. The U.S. agricultural sector now consists of a relatively small number of workers on farms, supported by many more upstream input suppliers and downstream processors and transporters. For every worker still employed today on American farms, there is approximately one upstream worker (supplying fertilizer or farm machinery) and as many as six downstream workers (storing, transporting, processing, and marketing farm products).[8] These upstream and downstream workers, who are an important part of the economic well-being of rural America, operate at a low margin with large fixed costs. They depend upon a high volume of business to survive. Massive mandatory farm production controls would devastate their income and employment prospects.

By one USDA estimate, a supply reduction on the scale envisioned by the Harkin-Gephardt bill (a 125-million-acre reduction, designed to raise commodity prices to 80 percent of parity) would so drastically reduce the volume of product moving through the larger agricultural system that it would cut upstream activity by $12 billion, and downstream activity by $35 billion. As many as 415,000 jobs would be lost upstream (especially in the fertilizer, farm equipment, and farm chemical industries), and as many as 1.1 million jobs would be lost downstream (in transport, storage, and processing industries). Furthermore, as much as $18 billion and 660,000 jobs would be lost on farms themselves.[9] Total job losses in the entire farm production sector might actually exceed the existing total number of U.S. farmers.

Unfortunately, this is just the beginning. The supply-management approach would also do considerable damage beyond the agriculture sector. Higher farm commodity prices would place a hidden and highly regressive tax on U.S. domestic food consumers. By one estimate, the Harkin-Gephardt plan would increase the retail price of bread by 12 percent, milk by 49 percent, poultry by 15 percent, pork by 36 percent, and beef by 12 percent. By 1991, the portion of domestic income spent on food would increase by 12 percent for middle-income U.S. households.[10]

Consumers abroad would also face higher U.S. commodity prices, but their reaction would simply be to stop buying from the United States, turning instead to competing suppliers. According to USDA estimates, export demand for U.S. farm commodities could fall immediately by as much as 40 percent. The result would be another loss of 250,000 American jobs and a further $10 billion reduction in GNP. Eventually, American consumers would also turn to foreign sources of supply. To prevent them from doing so, it might be necessary to put steep border tariffs or quota restrictions on all agricultural imports. Without such restrictions, U.S. millers and livestock producers in the Midwest might start importing their grain from Canada.

The sponsors of the Harkin-Gephardt approach have belatedly come to recognize some of these difficulties, and have amended their original proposal so as to include a variety of subsidies intended to compensate consumers, protect livestock producers, and help sustain exports. To protect U.S. trade interests, the bill now calls for the improbable negotiation of a worldwide market-sharing cartel agreement. If such an agreement could not be reached (within nine months), export subsidies would be used. Unfortunately, the accumulated budget cost of providing all the subsidies necessary to offset the damage done by supply management would eventually make this approach just as costly to taxpayers as the 1985 farm bill.

In a competitive world market, unilateral "supply management" by the United States provides a commercial bonanza for undeserving and less efficient agricultural producers abroad. They would enjoy the benefits of U.S. production restraint—the higher world prices—without having to curtail any of their own output. U.S. farmers cannot hope to compete while letting their own cropland go fallow. When cropland is idled, the fixed costs associated with owning that land do not disappear. Instead, they are simply spread over a smaller total output, causing both needless increases in production costs and reduced U.S. competitiveness. A unilateral decision to idle productive resources will convert competitive low-cost U.S. farmers into uncompetitive high-cost farmers. The foreign producers who would benefit are no doubt wishing the Harkin-Gephardt plan every success.

Since the costs and dangers are so clear, legislative movement in the direction of mandatory production controls appears, at this writing, most unlikely. During the 1985 farm bill debate, a production-control amendment offered by Rep. Berkley Bedell (D-Iowa) was defeated on the House floor by a wide margin.[11] Many influential farm groups are opposed to mandatory controls—including the American Farm Bureau Federation—and even if they were enacted by Congress, they could still be vetoed by the President, or by the farmers themselves in a binding referendum. Then again, mandatory controls do not have to be enacted into law to damage U.S. farm trade interests. Simply by continuing to debate controls, Congress calls into question the determination of the United States to persevere in its recent efforts to assume a more competitive agricultural trading posture abroad. Foreign governments watching this debate are given reason to keep their own farm subsidy programs in operation a little longer, with the hope that the United States will revert into a posture of unilateral agricultural disarmament.

Decoupling

For those who believe that unilateral supply management carries unacceptable costs and risks, and for those who do not yet wish to launch a direct assault against high target prices, a third approach to improving the 1985 farm bill presents itself. Through a "decoupling" of income-support payments from farm production decisions, production distortions could be reduced at an acceptable political cost, and without directly undermining farm income.

Under the current target price system, farmers must plant a crop to become eligible for deficiency payments. This link between payments and production encourages some relatively inefficient farmers to continue planting crops currently in surplus. If income-support payments could be provided to farmers without the accompanying requirement that crops be planted, the stimulus to unneeded production by less efficient farmers could be reduced.

A preliminary attempt to "decouple" payments from production decisions was actually made in the 1985 farm bill, under the so-called "50–92 provision." Farmers were given the right to collect deficiency payments on 92 percent of their permitted acreage, while planting only 50 percent of their eligible land.[12] Little use was made of this provision during the 1986 crop year, in part because of the large setup costs associated with planting any portion—even just 50 percent—of a farmer's acreage. Once those costs have been incurred, there may be few reasons to stop planting.[13] As a consequence, early in 1987 the administration proposed to make decoupling more effective through the enact-ment of a "0–92 provision," which would entitle farmers to defi-ciency payments even if they planted no land. This proposal fell short of what could be called "complete decoupling," since it in-cluded a stipulation that forbade farmers from switching to *non-program* crops on the land being idled. Under complete decoup-ling, farmers would receive payments while deciding what and how much to plant entirely upon the basis of market signals.

Complete decoupling has the long-run potential to eliminate both kinds of production distortions caused by the target price deficiency payment system. Inefficient farmers could receive payments without planting, and efficient farmers could accept payments without being forced to take good land out of produc-tion through "set asides." Under complete decoupling, the gov-ernment would be making payments to farmers not in return for their specific actions as producers, but instead for the purpose of supporting their endangered income, and for the social benefit that will accompany their continued presence on the land. Farm-ers could thus retain their current entitlement to public support, while recapturing their freedom to farm more efficiently in re-sponse to market forces. The resulting efficiency gains would strengthen further the competitive position of U.S. farm prod-ucts in world markets.

Complete decoupling also contains some possible drawbacks. First, greater freedom from government constraints on produc-tion could lead farmers simply to farm more, with no attention to increased efficiency. Some will continue planting even though their variable costs of production might be higher than free mar-ket prices, either to hold on to their farming lifestyle or to "pro-tect their base" (this would be an important motive if farmers saw decoupling only as a temporary experiment). Many relative-ly inefficient producers are known to stay in farming long after it has ceased to be profitable. They keep working their land "until the money runs out," simply out of a sense of personal or emo-tional attachment.[14] By putting more cash into the pockets of farmers, complete decoupling might fall prey to this tendency.

Second, many farmers are resistant to decoupling because it looks too much like welfare. For the sake of personal pride, farmers will want to continue to believe that they are receiving income support from the government in return for their efforts as producers. There are also more practical political reasons behind their desire to preserve "coupled" payments. If farm income-support programs were cashed out like welfare programs, they might become more visible and more vulnerable, as are welfare programs, to budget reductions.

One comprehensive proposal for complete decoupling which goes out of its way to avoid this welfare stigma is the Boschwitz-Boren Bill, a bipartisan measure co-sponsored by Senators Rudy Boschwitz (R-Mn.) and David Boren (D-Okla.). This measure would provide generous decoupled cash payments to farmers as a part of a "transition" to market-oriented farming. These "transition payments," which farmers could get purely on the basis of past acreage and yield, would be extremely generous at the outset (calculated to prevent any first year loss of farm income above variable costs), but would gradually decline as farm economy adjustments take place. After five years the transition payments would fall to only half of their original level.

The Boschwitz-Boren plan resembles an "adjustment assistance" program for farmers, rather than a permanent welfare scheme. Its long-range objective is a more efficient pattern of U.S. farm production, but it recognizes that movement toward that goal will impose adjustment costs on some producers. Farm producers who have been obliged for years to make production decisions and investments on the basis of highly intrusive government farm programs will need help in making the adjustment to a more liberal system. Generous cash payments to farmers, therefore, become justified in the short run as a means for buying adjustments that will make those expenditures less necessary in the long run.

The Boschwitz-Boren bill also accepts the need to "target" income-support payments more carefully toward middle-sized family farms, which the American people consider socially valuable and which are now under financial stress. This is in contrast to the current practice, which is to provide cash payments to farmers—up to $50,000 per farm—on an essentially untargeted basis. Some big farmers have been able to evade even this high $50,000 limit through subdivisions of land or sales to family members. Some recent programs have provided no cap on payments at all. The results have been scandalous. One-third of all payments have been granted to large farms with gross sales over $250,000, while nearly half of those farmers under severe financial stress receive nothing.

One final attraction to the Boschwitz-Boren approach is its compatibility with prudent soil and land conservation policy. The current "set-aside" approach takes land out of production, but not necessarily on the basis of erodability, and has given producers an unfortunate incentive to overapply fertilizers and pesticides on their remaining permitted acreage in order to increase the "base yields" used to compute government payments. A decoupling plan that refers only to historical acreage and yields would eliminate this undesirable incentive. A Conservation Reserve Program (CRP) for highly erodable lands was written into the 1985 farm bill. When it was first enacted, however, it did not attract sufficient participation in part because farmers were inadvertently given a stronger incentive in the form of high target prices to keep their land in the traditional programs. Participation began increasing in 1987, but this was largely due to offers of higher government rental payments. Under a complete decoupling plan, a conservation reserve would not be forced to bid against target price incentives to attract participation. A decoupling plan which gives farmers the opportunity to place highly erodable land in a conservation reserve also helps to alleviate the fear that farmers would be stigmatized as welfare recipients.

Given the benefit of hindsight, it is ironic that most of the opposition to the Boschwitz-Boren approach during the 1985 farm bill debate was due to its projected "high cost" to taxpayers.[15] The Congressional Budget Office estimated that it might cost $51 billion over the first three years, which seemed at the time much more than taxpayers could possibly afford. In view of the actual $25.8 billion *first year* cost of the legislative package enacted in 1985, this estimated price tag for the Boschwitz-Boren transition payment alternative no longer seems quite so lavish. If the cash outlays actually made during the first year after passage of the 1985 farm bill had been calculated and issued under a Boschwitz-Boren formula instead, taxpayers would have gotten more for their money. Benefits to farmers would have been targeted more carefully, fewer production distortions would have created in the U.S. farm economy, and the first and most difficult year of "transition" to a more competitive and genuinely market-oriented U.S. agricultural policy would have already been completed.[16]

The most significant problem with the 1985 farm bill is its burden on the budget. The risk is that budget officials, now facing a need to cut farm program spending, will either abandon the most attractive feature in the 1985 farm bill—lower commodity loan rates—or fall into the trap of "supply management," propping up world prices for competitors abroad through massive acreage reductions at home. Unfortunately, supply management could creep in even without a major change in current legislation. In 1987, simply by using the considerable authority contained in the 1985 farm bill, budget-conscious officials decreased total U.S. corn, wheat, and soybean acreage to the lowest levels seen since the 1983 PIK program. These acreage reductions are nonetheless combined with the intensive use of inputs on the remaining land. This means an opportunity is still being lost to make U.S. agriculture more competitive, by allowing farmers the freedom to adopt an extensive and less distorted production mode. It also means the full trade potential of the U.S. farm sector is still going to waste.

The Trade Consequences of Domestic Farm Policy Reform

Just what is the full trade potential of the U.S. farm sector? The lower loan rates contained in the 1985 farm bill were designed in part to test that potential. Lower U.S. loan rates should be both a stimulus to importers abroad, and a deterrent to competing foreign producers and exporters. World trade should grow more rapidly, and the U.S. share of that trade should increase.

Past experience suggests that the trade benefit from market-oriented commodity loan rates can be substantial. During the 1950s, as in the 1980s, there were doubts about the commercial export potential of American farming. Export growth was sluggish, being sustained largely through shipments of "food aid" to poor countries at the taxpayer's expense. The U.S. share of world wheat exports sagged from 39 percent in 1949–52 to only 29 percent by 1953–55. There was a widespread preoccupation then, as now, with "surplus production capacity." The real problem was high price guarantees. The same high domestic commodity loan rates that were generating the production surplus were also pricing U.S. farm goods out of world markets.

Only when the U.S. eventually began to reduce its domestic commodity loan rates—and hence its export prices—did commercial trade prospects finally begin to brighten. From the early 1950s up to the 1968–72 period, with considerable political effort, the price support for U.S. wheat was gradually reduced in real terms by more than 60 percent, eventually bringing U.S. export prices more in line with world market forces. This shift toward greater market orientation was controversial since some farmers experienced as much as a 40–50 percent reduction in guaranteed returns per bushel of production over this period, even with their direct payments factored in. By the early 1970s, however, the strategy began to pay off handsomely, in part because dollar exchange rates finally came down as well. By 1973, both U.S. agricultural exports and farm income were soaring to record levels. World grain trade doubled during the 1970s, and thanks to competitive pricing, U.S. exporters captured three-quarters of the new business. What had once looked like "excess production capacity" in the U.S. agriculture sector had now became a valuable commercial asset in an environment of expanding world farm trade.

Unrealistic expectations generated during the 1970s commodity boom soon caused U.S. domestic price-support levels, unfortunately, to begin creeping up again. Politicians courted farm votes with large election-year loan rate increases in both 1976 and 1980. Then in the 1981 farm bill, because inflation was expected to continue, future target prices were set on a rigid upward trajectory. Long-term trends in commodity price supports should have been downward, because of farm productivity growth. By 1982–85, however, real price-support levels for U.S. wheat were back up to 20 percent above the levels of 1968–72. Target prices for wheat were higher in real terms in 1985 than they had been in 1974. Under the cover of the 1970s commodity price boom, the United States had allowed its own domestic support levels to move up too high, and to get in the way of both domestic adjustment and export expansion once that boom came to an end.[17] It was to correct this error that the 1985 farm bill gave the Secretary of Agriculture so much authority to reduce domestic commodity loan rates.

It is still too early to judge with confidence when the 1986 relowering of commodity loan rates will begin to produce convincing trade benefits. Early disappointments had to be expected, not only because it took most of a year for the announcement of lower loan rates to translate into reduced export prices, but also because it can take even longer for production and trade actions by foreign customers and competitors to adjust to lower prices. Damage done by years of uncompetitive export pricing does not disappear overnight. Foreign customers do not instantly adjust consumption and trade patterns, and foreign competitors with recently expanded production capacities and large carryover stocks do not back out of markets in a single season.

In the long run, lower U.S. prices will stimulate more total foreign demand, and more demand for U.S. products in particular, leading to a growth in export revenues. But getting to the long run takes patience. Export demand in agricultural markets can be price *inelastic* in the short run, meaning that for at least a year or so a fall in export prices will produce a less than proportionate increase in sales volume. During this difficult transitional period export volume may increase, but because of lower prices, total export revenues will actually fall. As of early 1987, U.S. agriculture had yet to emerge from this difficult short-run period of adjustment. The total volume of U.S. exports was beginning to increase in response to lower export prices, but total export value was still depressed. World wheat and coarse grain trade increased roughly 6 percent in 1986/1987, after having fallen by 7 percent a year from 1981 to 1985. U.S. exports grew in terms of volume by 22 percent.[18] U.S. rice exports were up 50 percent and cotton exports were more than triple those of the previous marketing year. However, the lower prices that were helping to stimulate this volume growth kept total export values momentarily in check.

As a word of caution, when an upturn in the value as well as the total volume of U.S. agricultural exports is eventually noted, lower domestic commodity loan rates will deserve only part of the credit. Much lower dollar exchange rates since 1985—particularly against both the Japanese yen and the ECU—will also have played a significant role, just as they did in the 1970s. Export subsidy programs, such as the EEP, will likewise have been a factor. Ideally, U.S. farmers should be relying on their own high productivity rather than on government subsidies to generate competitive export prices. Yet, with so many production controls currently in place at home, some level of subsidy can perhaps be excused as an offsetting means to create a fully competitive price posture abroad. Overall rates of income growth overseas are one other important variable in the export performance equation. The trade effects of lower U.S. loan rates can be greatly enhanced (as in the 1970s) or largely nullified by sudden fluctuations in the larger macroeconomic environment.

With all of these provisos in mind, and despite the brief period of time in question, there is still plenty of evidence to suggest that the "market-oriented" loan rates contained in the 1985 farm bill are beginning to produce healthy production and trade effects abroad. This is most evident in the evolving production response of several key export competitors. Because many of these export competitors have relatively large stocks on hand, their *trade* response to lower U.S. export prices cannot develop immediately. They may spend more on export subsidies as necessary in the short run to reduce their stock burden. But such export subsidies quickly become burdensome to developing country competitors, which have limited budget resources, and also to some wealthy competitors such as Canada and Australia, which export a large share of total production. To reduce subsidy burdens, these competitors cut back on acreage expansion and reduce production incentives at home.

Evidence suggests that this healthy process is already underway. In Canada, Australia, and Argentina, total grain exports and total harvested grain acreage increased steadily throughout the 1970s and continued to do so well into the early 1980s because high dollar exchange rates and noncompetitive U.S. farm policies were propping up world prices. Between 1979 and 1983, harvested grain area in the three countries increased by 25 percent, and exports rose by 33 percent. Now, at last, this increase in both acreage and exports has been brought to a halt. In 1986, largely in response to lower world prices, these three competitors reduced their total grain acreage by 8 percent and their total exports by 11 percent from the earlier peak level.[19] By early 1987, the Australian Wheat Board was expecting wheat plantings to fall at least 20 percent below the 1983–84 peak level, and Argentine wheat plantings were expected to decrease 28 percent from 1983–84. Canadian plantings were also forecast to decline in 1987 as the government announced an initial wheat price to farmers 15 percent below the 1986–87 level. This price reduction was needed to lower escalating internal budget costs and to keep Canadian wheat competitive with relatively inexpensive U.S. wheat in foreign markets.[20]

Predictably, Canadian and Australian farmers have complained loudly about having to make these difficult adjustments in response to lower U.S. export prices. To the degree that lower U.S. export prices are a result of direct EEP subsidies, they have a point. On the other hand, to the extent that today's lower prices simply reflect more market-oriented U.S. domestic loan rates, protests from competitors should be discounted. Foreign trade rivals were given a free ride by high U.S. loan rates for too long. Between 1981 and 1985, when the United States was propping up world prices, cutting back acreage, and carrying larger stocks, its share of world wheat markets fell from 48 percent all the way down to 29 percent. At the same time, in Canada, Australia, and Argentina, both acreage and production were expanding, and their joint share of world wheat markets increased from 32.4 percent up to 45.4 percent. U.S. farm exporters do not have to apologize for belatedly using more competitive loan rates and dollar exchange rates to correct these adverse trends.

Of greater importance in the long run will be the reaction of the EC to these more competitive U.S. export prices. As a much more lavish export subsidizer—in part because it is still less dependent on exports than either Canada or Australia—the EC will probably be slow to discipline its internal price and production policies in response to the external market realities created by lower U.S. commodity loan rates. There are nonetheless signs that such a response may be building.

Lower U.S. export prices, caused by lower loan rates and dollar exchange rates, have obliged the EC to begin spending much more on export restitutions simply to stay in line with world market prices. When U.S. wheat export prices suddenly became more competitive in 1986, EC wheat export-restitution payments had to increase, moving sharply upward from 20 ECUs per ton to 140 ECUs per ton in just 18 months time. In part because of these much larger export costs per ton, Community restitutions were momentarily suspended after April 1987, and exports (at least for the moment) slowed their increase. EC-12 wheat and flour exports for 1986/87 were forecast to remain steady at just 15 million tons, which is actually below the 1982/83–1984/85 average of 16.8 million tons.[21]

Distracted by escalating trans-Atlantic farm trade tensions and continuing export subsidy battles, it has been easy to miss these underlying indications of EC restraint. It should not be surprising, however, that even the CAP must make adjustments when it encounters suddenly altered international market conditions. The tragedy is that U.S. agricultural policy for so long helped the EC to postpone these adjustments. As late as 1983, because of high dollar exchange rates and noncompetitive U.S. export prices, the net cost to the EC budget of running its grain import and export programs was actually *negative*. The EC was then still collecting more on import levies than it was spending on export subsidies. It was not until 1986, when a newly competitive world market environment suddenly pushed up grain export-restitution costs, that these trading programs began costing the EC budget dearly. Expenditures went from a *negative* $61 million in 1983 up to a *positive* $700 million in 1986.[22] In February 1987 the Community reported that total farm budget spending for the new year would have to go up by another 1.8 billion ECU (about $2 billion) due to the continuing decline in the dollar price of international agricultural products.[23] One result has been a belated but nonetheless healthy stimulus to policy reform.

The impetus to reform that comes from larger EC restitution costs should not be exaggerated. Export-restitution outlays for cereals still amount to only a small share (about 13 percent) of total Community restitution payments, which, in turn, are only about one-third of total expenditures under the European Agricultural Guidance and Guarentee Fund (EAGGF).[24] Moreover, these expenditures have shown a consistent ability to expand, having grown from annual levels of around 5 billion ECU in the mid-1970s to a level of roughly 21 billion ECU by 1986. The Community has had to negotiate its way through repeated farm budget crises in order to achieve this expansion, but it is fortunate to have abundant economic resources at its disposal. In 1985 the same farm support expenditures that took up roughly two-thirds of the EC budget, took up only *two-thirds of 1 percent* of total Community GDP.[25]

The Community also has powerful revenue instruments at its disposal to tap these resources. Roughly 60 percent of EC budget revenues are now collected through VAT contributions from member countries, and it takes only a small relative increase in these contributions to produce a large revenue gain. In 1985 the Community was able to boost its potential revenues by 40 percent, through a relatively inconspicuous increase (from 1 percent up to 1.4 percent) in the maximum member-country VAT contributions. The new revenues, originally authorized to cover the anticipated costs of Community enlargement, were practically exhausted by the time those costs were just beginning to be felt in 1986. Additional revenue gains are likely in 1988, however, when the VAT contribution cap might well be increased up to 1.6 percent.

Despite such means of resilience, there is still plenty of evidence that high farm budget costs inside the EC can be a useful stimulus to internal CAP reform. Significant proposals for CAP reform of the Guarantee section were first widely circulated inside the Community in the late 1970s in response to a Commission projection that the EAGGF was soon to run out of money. These forecasts would have been accurate—and serious agricultural reforms might have been undertaken in the early 1980s—had it not been for the slowdown in CAP operating expenses brought on both by high dollar exchange rates and by high U.S. commodity loan rates. The impetus to reform was then lost, not to re-emerge until the budget ceiling was finally reached in 1983–84.[26]

The reappearance of acute CAP budget problems in 1983–84 finally compelled the Community to adopt a significant set of internal agricultural policy reforms. In March 1984 the dairy sector was brought under improved cost control through an imposition of production quotas, a step the Community had never been willing to take before. A harsh "super-levy" penalty was exacted on those who exceeded their quota, and Community milk production was for the first time reduced. Budget constraints also encouraged the Community to embrace much lower grain export-restitution payments in 1984. At one point late in the year, despite a record domestic cereals harvest which meant excessively large carryover stocks, EC wheat export-restitution payments were briefly reduced to zero. Exceptionally high dollar exchange rates were at that time rendering U.S. wheat exports entirely noncompetitive, so this money-saving no-subsidy policy almost worked for the Community. It was significant that the Community was using noncompetitive U.S. export prices as a means to relieve budget stress at home, rather than as an opportunity to continue expanding its export shares abroad.

Under growing budget pressures the Community also took several other reform measures in 1984 that carried implied benefits for U.S. agriculture. Community prices for all commodities were actually *reduced* for the first time in history, by a nominal 0.5 percent in ECU terms. Due to simultaneous adjustments in the complicated EC agrimonetary system, this nominal decrease was something of an illusion—translated into national currencies, it was actually a 2.9 percent increase—but this was still below the prevailing rate of inflation. An effort was also made to place tighter limits on future cereals price increases. A "guarantee threshold" was established for cereals which linked price increases inversely to actual production trends. If it had worked properly, it would have required cereals prices in 1985–86 to be cut by 5 percent, from whatever level would have otherwise been set. Unfortunately, this measure was blocked by a German veto within the Council of Ministers, but the Commission nonetheless went forward to administer a 1.8 percent cereals price cut on its own authority. Cereals price discipline was also enforced unilaterally by the Commission through tighter limits on the timing of its intervention purchases.

This budget-induced momentum toward internal CAP reform has now been accelerated considerably due to the even greater pressures that are growing out of lower U.S. dollar exchange rates and commodity loan rates. Soon after U.S. loan rates reductions were announced in 1986, the Council of Ministers responded by keeping overall EC farm support price levels essentially frozen, reducing support prices for low-quality wheat, and imposing on cereal growers a new 3 percent "co-responsibility levy," to offset some of the larger cost of export restitutions. In December 1986, still under budget pressure, the Council of Ministers agreed to reduce milk production quotas by 9.5 percent over two years and to lower support prices for beef by 12 percent. Early in 1987 the Community went on to announce new reductions in storage payments to farmers, a further tightening of wheat quality controls, further limitations on intervention purchases and continued "restrictive" pricing.

These constructive steps toward greater internal EC farm policy discipline have all been taken in response to internal budget pressures. Financial pressures do not always push proposed EC policy changes in the right direction, as the 1987 revival of a fats and oils tax proposal so clearly indicates. In most instances, however, the direction of change has been toward internal price and production restraint, which is good for U.S. farmers, not to mention EC consumers and taxpayers. Positive movement on reform was probably inevitable inside the CAP, once the Community began transforming itself, in one market after another, from a net importer into a net exporter of farm products. U.S. policy, however, can also have an influence. The export-restitution costs and other budget pressures which push reforms forward have been at least an indirect function of U.S. domestic commodity loan rates and dollar exchange rates. Holding on to competitive commodity loan rates in the United States is one of the best ways possible to ensure continued movement toward greater farm policy discipline inside the EC.

To encourage greater EC discipline in this fashion, the actual size of the added budget pressure created by competitive U.S. prices may not be as important as the certainty that it will continue. If the EC can be persuaded that in future years the United States will not revert to its earlier habit of propping up world prices through the unilateral imposition of high loan rates, or through 1983 PIK-style production controls, then advocates of reform in Brussels will have a stronger hand to play. If, on the other hand, EC farm interests are given reason to hope that the United States might soon lapse back into its earlier posture of high price guarantees and massive unilateral production controls, a policy of "no change" will begin to appear affordable, and the politically difficult task of CAP reform will again be postponed.

This sort of persistent pressure for reform, imposed on the Community in a nonprovocative fashion through market forces and internal budget mechanisms, can also make the early success of a GATT negotiation on agriculture that much more likely. It is no accident that international interest in a multilateral agricultural negotiation began to increase in 1986, precisely when U.S. commodity loan rates and dollar exchange rates began their sharp decline. Additional U.S. domestic agricultural policy reforms, such as target price reductions and an eventual shift to targeted and decoupled "transition payments," could add still more to the likely success of these international negotiations. Target price reductions would make competitive export pricing more affordable to U.S. taxpayers, and hence a more sustainable pressure tactic. Decoupled payments would protect the United States, in Geneva, from EC charges that current income-support measures are trade distorting.

Some may argue that additional reforms in U.S. domestic agricultural policy should be taken only *after* a final GATT agreement has been concluded. To take any domestic reform actions outside of GATT would be to unilaterally give away our "bargaining chips," without receiving any immediate quid pro quo in return. Those who hold this view fail to appreciate that U.S. bargaining leverage in Geneva will be enhanced rather than weakened by domestic reforms which put added price and budget pressure on foreign competitors. It is by *not* taking such reforms that the United States will disarm itself in Geneva. Those who talk about postponing such reforms in order to preserve "bargaining chips" in GATT are playing into the hands of protectionist farm groups at home that are opposed to reform under any circumstances, and which have little or no interest in a successful GATT negotiation.

Not all badly needed U.S. domestic farm policy reforms, if taken unilaterally, would place added price or budget pressures on foreign competitors. U.S. cereals policy reforms may be the exception rather than the rule. If the United States were to liberalize its sugar and dairy policies unilaterally, without waiting for GATT, foreign competitors such as the EC would gain some additional leeway to hold their own illiberal sugar and dairy policies in place. In such circumstances, the question of how far to go in the direction of unilateral reform becomes more difficult. Does it make sense to refrain from taking reforms which could bring unambiguous domestic social benefits, simply because foreigners are not yet ready to follow? It is said by GATT enthusiasts that the promise of a multilateral agreement will be the only way to make reform acceptable to U.S. producer interests. But GATT has yet to produce much for dairy or sugar. Where multilateral agreements can speed up the reform process, they should be vigorously pursued. Where they risk being used by producer groups as an excuse to postpone reform, they should be approached with caution, and more emphasis should be placed on unilateral reform. Fortunately for the United States, in some important product areas (such as cereals policy), both the multilateral and the unilateral reform processes can be pursued simultaneously, and can be used to reinforce one another.

Notes

1. Technically, the farmer first "pawns" his surplus commodities to the CCC, in return for a "loan" of cash. If market prices do not improve, however, he is free to keep the cash, and the CCC is left owning the commodities.
2. The "market price" is calculated as the average price received by farmers over the first five months of the marketing year.
3. The Democratic-controlled House of Representatives originally demanded a four-year freeze. Even the Republican-controlled Senate embraced a freeze of shorter duration, despite the objections of Agriculture Committee Chairman Jesse Helms (R-NC). Republican ranks within the Senate Agricultural Committee were broken on the target price issue when Senator Mark Andrews (R-ND) voted with the Democrats to keep target prices high. Andrews was just one of many vulnerable Senate Republicans in farm states up for re-election in 1986. In the end he was defeated anyway, despite his decision to break ranks with the administration on farm programs in 1985.
4. *Economic Report of the President 1987, op. cit.*, p. 156.
5. Ibid., p. 172.
6. "Defeat Expected for Plan to Cut Crop Target Prices," *Journal of Commerce*, February 10, 1987, p. 12A.

7. Parity is a measure of the purchasing power of agricultural products versus nonagricultural products from an antiquated 1910–14 base period.

8. David Harrington, Gerald Schluter, and Patrick O'Brien, "Agriculture's Links to the National Economy," U.S. Department of Agriculture, Economic Research Service, *Agriculture Information Bulletin*, no. 504 (October 1986).

9. Ibid.

10. "The 1985 Farm Bill Revisited: Midcourse Corrections or Stay the Course," Briefing Book, National Center for Food and Agricultural Policy, Resources for the Future, Washington, April 1987.

11. Supporters of mandatory controls did manage at the last minute to insert into the 1985 farm bill a requirement that the USDA conduct a *nonbinding* referendum among wheat growers, to sample their attitudes toward mandatory production controls. When the referendum was administered the following July, it revealed that 54 percent of the wheat growers responding wanted mandatory controls. Even though the valid response rate was much too low (24 percent) to be conclusive, Senator Harkin nonetheless labeled it as "a major repudiation of the Reagan Administration's farm program," and an important endorsement—by the producers themselves—of his supply-control alternative.

12. Permitted acreage is defined as the acreage that remains after land has been idled under an acreage-reduction program.

13. *Economic Report of the President 1987, op. cit.*, p. 155.

14. The tendency for farmers to stay on the land long after they could be earning a better income off the farm has frustrated many efforts to facilitate efficient adjustments in the agricultural sector. One 1986 survey of North Dakota farmers shows that roughly two-thirds of those who finally left the land in the early 1980s ended up better off financially. See *Agweek*, April 20, 1987, p. 56.

15. The high-cost argument set the administration against the Boschwitz-Boren approach and ensured its eventual defeat, although it did in the end receive the symbolic approval of forty-two Senators in a final sympathy vote on the floor of the Senate.

16. Some critics reject the Boschwitz-Boren approach because they doubt that the promised reduction of transition payments would ever take place. As originally introduced, the bill contained a loophole provision which allowed the Secretary of Agriculture to continue offering transition payments at the 100 percent level, if he deemed that circumstances were not right for a phase-out.

17. D. Gale Johnson, "Broadening the Horizon," in *U.S. Agricultural Exports and Third World Development: The Critical Linkage*, an Agricultural Policy Study of the Curry Foundation, Conference Papers and Materials, Washington, July 14–15, 1986.

18. U.S. Department of Agriculture, "World Grain Situation and Outlook," FG-6-87 (May 1987), pp. 1–12.

19. U.S. Department of Agriculture, "World Grain Situation and Outlook," FG-4-87 (March 1987), p. 7.

20. *U.S. Wheat Associates Letter*, April 24, 1987.

21. U.S. Department of Agriculture, "World Grain Situation and Outlook," FG-5-87 (April 1987), p. 8.

22. Commission of the European Communities, "Commission Proposals on the Prices for Agricultural Products and on Related Measures (1987/1988)," vol. II, Com (87) 1 final, Brussels, 24 February 1987, p. 6.

23. Statement submitted by Carroll G. Brunthaver before the Senate Agricultural Subcommittee on Foreign Agricultural Policy, July 29, 1986.

24. In 1985, cereals restitutions were appropriated at about 1 billion ECU, while total restitutions were appropriated at 7.9 billion ECU. See Donna U. Vogt and Jasper Womach, "Tensions in United States-European Community Agricultural Trade," U.S. Library of Congress, Congressional Research Service, Report No. 86-112 ENR, May 16, 1986, p. CRS-30.

25. Ruth Elleson, "The EC Budget: Implications for the CAP," U.S. Department of Agriculture, Economic Research Service, October 1986. (Unpublished.)

26. Stefan Tangermann, "Special Features and Ongoing Reforms of the CAP," in Randall B. Purcell, ed., *Confrontation or Negotiation: United States Policy and European Agriculture* (New York: Associated Faculty Press, 1985), p. 96.

Five

In Conclusion: Beyond Farm Trade Policy

We have seen that fixing farm trade will require a proper mix of actions in at least three separate agricultural policy settings—within GATT, in the international arena outside of GATT, and in domestic agricultural policy.

In GATT, the current Uruguay Round must be used to tighten existing agricultural trade rules, to consider a variety of trade expanding bilateral bargains, and to build international consensus for genuine subsidy reductions. Merely seeking a subsidy freeze, which is difficult to measure and enforce, will not be enough, given both current high levels of agricultural protection and the tendency of farm productivity growth to render any fixed level of protection increasingly disruptive over time.

Outside of GATT, the United States must take care to avoid international commodity agreements which protect foreign competitors by rigging prices or freezing existing market shares. Such agreements tend to tie the hands of low-cost U.S. farmers, which is precisely why so many high-cost foreign competitors are in favor of them. The United States would also be well-advised to avoid falling into an open-ended and mutually destructive agricultural trade war. Since the United States is still the world's largest agricultural exporter, it would have to spend the most on export subsidies and risk the greatest loss of market access, simply to stay even in such a war.

In its domestic agricultural policies, the United States should hold on to those features of the 1985 farm bill, such as market-oriented loan rates, which aid competitive export pricing, while making adjustments in other elements of the bill, such as high target prices, which break the budget. High budget costs place the future competitiveness of U.S. agricultural exports at risk because they tempt policy officials back into the dangerous expedient of unilateral production controls. A better way to support income and encourage efficient adjustment in the financially stressed U.S. farm sector is to decouple payments to farmers from production decisions. American taxpayers have demonstrated their willingness to provide generous income support to farmers in trouble. It is time to give them their money's worth by providing this support in a more intelligent manner.

Appropriate U.S. agricultural policy actions must be taken in all three of these settings *simultaneously*. Liberal domestic agricultural policy reforms which are desirable on their own terms should not be held up while waiting for multilateral agreements to be negotiated in GATT. By taking such domestic policy reforms promptly, the United States in some instances will be able to create more sustained international market pressures, which will in turn generate more sustained budget pressures inside foreign governments, and thereby make the successful negotiation of a GATT agreement that much more likely. At the very least, U.S. trade negotiators must begin to build greater domestic political support for agricultural policy changes; otherwise they will lack credibility when they start talking about "swapping reforms" in Geneva.

Veterans of agricultural policymaking will recognize this as a demanding agenda. Agricultural policy reforms, however, are only one part of an overall prescription for fixing farm trade. Nonagricultural policy actions are essential as well, given the sensitivity of international farm trade to disruptions in the larger macroeconomic environment. This brief concluding chapter will provide just a partial inventory of the nonfarm policy actions that are necessary if U.S. agriculture is ever to realize its full trade potential. These measures include more disciplined and more consistent fiscal and monetary policies, more liberal manufacturing trade policies, and more generous international financial and foreign assistance policies.

Fiscal and Monetary Policy

As described in Chapter 1, fluctuations in agricultural trade tend to grow out of the fluctuating macroeconomic environment, which is heavily influenced in turn by the conduct of U.S. fiscal and monetary policy. The disrupted conditions of world farm trade since the early 1970s have to a considerable extent been caused by a lack of U.S. fiscal policy discipline, plus a lack of U.S. monetary policy consistency. Inflationary boom and deflationary bust conditions in the global macroeconomy since the early 1970s, accompanied by wild swings in dollar exchange rates, have obliged U.S. farm exporters to make too many sudden and costly adjustments. Undisciplined U.S. budget policies, accompanied by changing monetary policies which go from loose to tight, have helped create this disruptive macroeconomic roller coaster. Until the roller coaster ride is brought to a halt by a restoration of macroeconomic policy discipline, the disruptions in international agricultural trade will continue.

Thus far in the 1980s the macroeconomic situation has been getting worse rather than better. In 1981 federal income tax rates were cut sharply, as an ill-conceived and short-sighted political gift to the voting public, but federal budget expenditures continued to soar. Between 1981 and 1986 defense spending and Medicare outlays almost doubled, and Social Security expenses increased by 45 percent. As a result, gross federal debt increased from 26 percent of GNP in 1980 to more than 40 percent of GNP by 1987. $140 billion must now be spent every year simply to pay the interest on this debt, a figure that will continue to increase so long as the deficit spending continues, adding still more to the deficit and, hence, to the debt.

Will the U.S. government eventually be forced, under threat of another recession, to inflate its way out of this domestic (and now foreign) indebtedness? What would such an inflation, and the still larger recession that might follow, do to agricultural commodity prices, interest rates, and currency exchange rates? U.S. agricultural producers and traders, who are just now beginning to recover from one painful cycle of boom and bust macroeconomic shock, would be put through the adjustment wringer a second time.

U.S. agricultural producers and their political spokesmen do not yet fully appreciate the powerful connections between fluctuating macroeconomic conditions and farm trade.[1] They feel more comfortable operating within the traditional confines of the narrow agricultural sector, pressuring the agricultural committees of the Congress to make marginal adjustments in the terms of their favorite commodity programs. Until U.S. agricultural interests begin to feel just as comfortable talking to the Federal Reserve Board about monetary policy, or speaking out on budget policy, they will be rowing upstream with only one oar in the water. Without a more stable macroeconomic environment, efforts by agricultural policy officials to fix farm trade will encounter repeated frustration.

Manufacturing Trade Policy

Those who wish to fix farm trade must also be ready to take appropriate parallel actions in the arena of nonfarm trade, including, especially, trade in manufactured products with the developing world. Growing protection of U.S. manufactured trade markets is emerging as a large and direct threat to the expansion of U.S. agricultural exports. Foreign trade partners with manufactured goods to sell, and especially those in the developing world with heavy external debts and difficulties in earning foreign exchange, cannot be expected to purchase more agricultural products from the United States—even in the most favorable macroeconomic environment—if U.S. borders are closed to their exports.

The importance of cultivating trade partners for U.S. agriculture in the developing world cannot be overemphasized. Most of the future growth in international farm markets will take place in the LDCs, where four-fifths of the world's citizens live, where population growth rates are still high, and where diets have so much room to improve. Already more than 40 percent of all U.S. farm exports go to the developing world, up from 30 percent just a decade ago. What makes the LDCs better customers for U.S. farm exports is broad-based income growth, and an ability either to earn or to borrow foreign exchange.[2] Increasingly, they are seeking foreign exchange earnings through international sales of low-technology or light manufactured products, such as steel, textiles, shoes, or consumer electronics. When the United States decides to protect its own less efficient domestic manufacturers in these markets, either with explicit tariffs and quotas or with more subtle devices such as "voluntary" trade restraints or cartel-like "Multifibre Arrangements," it prevents excluded LDCs from earning the income and foreign exchange necessary to become good customers for U.S. agricultural exports.

Sometimes this important link between U.S. manufactured trade protectionism and a loss of U.S. agricultural exports is made explicit, as when China retaliated in 1983 and 1984 against a sequence of unilateral U.S. textile import restraints by cancelling roughly $500 million in anticipated purchases of U.S wheat. More often, however, this connection has remained somewhat difficult for traditional political leaders and farm trade advocates to perceive, so they have yet to give full voice to their keen interest in the matter. One particularly dangerous incarnation of this protectionist urge is the so-called Gephardt amendment of 1987, a trade provision which would require retaliation against any country running excessive trade surpluses with the United States. This amendment targets countries such as Japan, South Korea, Taiwan, West Germany, and Brazil, all good customers for U.S. agricultural exports. Political leaders who preach protection for the less efficient parts of the U.S. manufacturing sector should be confronted, by agricultural leaders, with the damage this could do to U.S. farm trade.

International Financial Policy

Potential customers for U.S. agricultural exports in the developing world are not only threatened today by protectionist U.S. manufacturing trade policies. They are also burdened by an inadequate U.S. response to their recent international financial difficulties. Not unlike U.S. farmers, many LDC governments suddenly found themselves with unserviceable debts when they were surprised by a tightening of U.S. monetary policies, much higher interest rates, and the world recession of 1982. This debt problem has been most severe in Latin America, where the trade consequences for U.S. agriculture have been costly in two respects. First, in order to conserve foreign exchange, Latin American countries had to cut back sharply on their agricultural imports. Between 1981 and 1985, the total value of their agricultural imports from the United States declined by 33 percent.[3] Second, hoping to earn more foreign exchange, heavily indebted, but agriculturally powerful, Latin American countries such as Argentina have felt obliged to increase their own farm exports, at times in direct competition with U.S. agriculture. After 1981, while U.S. wheat and soybean exports were falling, Argentine wheat and soybean exports were on the rise.

When, in 1982, the Latin American debt problem hit crisis levels, the initial U.S. reaction was to embrace a long-standing practice of the International Monetary Fund (IMF) to reschedule unserviceable foreign debts on the condition these debtor governments impose new internal policies of "austerity." This shock-treatment approach not only cut income growth sharply in the short run; it also did little to encourage new investments to revive growth in the future. It did bring forth some new international lending, especially from the IMF itself, but many overexposed international commercial banks remained on the sidelines. Having helped create the crisis by lending too much, these banks made the crisis worse by lending too little and by insisting that all past loans continue to be serviced, despite the sudden change in macroeconomic circumstances. Total indebtedness continued to grow, as net capital outflows from debtor countries reached more than twice the level of net borrowing from the commercial banks.

It was not until 1985 that the U.S. government finally recognized the need for an international financial strategy that would give greater weight to reviving economic growth in Latin America. Late in that year, Treasury Secretary James A. Baker III proposed "A Program for Sustained Growth" which envisioned additional lending of $29 billion over three years—including $20 billion from commercial banks—to fifteen highly indebted countries, ten of which are in Latin America. To qualify for these loans the debtor country would have to undertake "comprehensive macroeconomic and structural reforms" designed to stimulate investment and growth. Baker argued that "there must be a commitment by the banking community—a commitment to help the global community make the necessary transition to stronger growth."[4] An alternative approach for moving U.S. international financial policy in a more growth-oriented direction was subsequently proposed by Senator Bill Bradley (D-NJ), who advocated outright debt relief. His plan calls for a 3 percentage point reduction in the interest rates, and forgives 3 percent of the principal over a three-year period.

U.S. international commercial banks have been cool to the Baker plan, not wanting to "throw good money after bad," and hostile to the Bradley plan, because it would cost them a loss in earnings. This is short-sighted. If a strategy is not quickly found to provide additional financial resources on more growth-oriented terms, the heavily indebted countries of Latin America will not only stop purchasing U.S. agricultural exports; they may also fail to maintain their interest payments to U.S. banks, as Brazil did beginning in early 1987. Those who wish to fix U.S. farm trade, with Latin America in particular, should encourage lending policies with more foresight from U.S. commercial banks.

Foreign Assistance Policy

Foreign aid represents a final nonfarm policy means to cultivate good customers for U.S. agriculture in the developing world. Where foreign assistance makes a direct contribution to income growth, and hence to larger dietary demands, it should be viewed by U.S. agriculturalists as a valuable tool for international farm market expansion.

It is no accident that some of today's largest developing country farm importers were once recipients of generous quantities of U.S. foreign aid. During the years following 1945, Taiwan and South Korea together received roughly $18.6 billion in U.S. economic and military aid.[5] This high level of assistance made higher internal rates of savings possible and contributed directly to agricultural and industrial development, eventually transforming Taiwan and South Korea into prosperous countries with increasing personal income and a growing appetite for imported food—especially animal feedstuffs to upgrade the meat content of the diet. Taiwan evolved, in the process, from a net exporter of cereals in the 1950s into a net importer of 60 percent of its much larger total cereals consumption today. No longer a recipient of U.S. foreign aid handouts, Taiwan now purchases more than $1 billion of U.S agricultural products every year on straight commercial terms. Taiwan and South Korea, despite their small population size, import more wheat and coarse grains every year than all of the "hungrier," and more populous, nations of Sub-Saharan Africa combined.

Those who wish to expand U.S. agricultural sales should therefore lament the continuing decline in the real dollar value of total U.S. development assistance to poor countries and the trivial level of effort that is now represented by that assistance. At a time when LDC income growth has become more important to U.S. agriculture, the federal government has decided to back out of its traditional leadership role in promoting Third World development. Twenty years ago the United States still gave 0.58 percent of its GNP every year to the developing world in foreign economic assistance. Today that figure is down to 0.24 percent. Among the seventeen major noncommunist nations that offer substantial economic assistance to the developing world, the United States stands seventeenth—dead last—in terms of aid effort.[6] U.S. agricultural export interests will be among the first to suffer if Third World development slows down. They should be taking the lead to reverse this sorry trend.

Prospects for Fixing Farm Trade

With all that has been said here about the need to push forward with international farm trade liberalization in GATT, to promote and to defend U.S. farm trade interests outside of GATT, to remedy the flaws in U.S. domestic farm legislation, to restore balance and discipline to U.S. macroeconomic policy, to resist protectionism in U.S. manufactured trade policy, and to adopt more generous growth-promoting international financial and assistance policies, it must be admitted that the task of fixing farm trade is a formidable one indeed. Political leaders will no doubt continue to duck away from this task whenever they are permitted to do so by their distracted or bewildered constituents.

It is the responsibility of U.S. political leaders and their constituents, both inside the agricultural community and beyond, to see more clearly the costs and risks of allowing the world's agricultural trading system to evade repair. The long-term prosperity of U.S. agriculture is at stake, and much more. Our purpose here has been to give those in the United States who have the courage to face up to this problem a better means to organize and inform their own thinking, so as to strengthen the push toward a desirable mix of policy solutions.

Notes

1. For one recent and authoritative review of these connections, see "U.S. Macroeconomic Policy and Agriculture," remarks by Robert L. Thompson, Assistant Secretary of Agriculture for Economics, U.S. Department of Agriculture/Universities Consortium for Agricultural Trade Research Conference, Tahoe City, California, July 24–26, 1986.
2. Quite often in the developing world this process of broad-based income growth must begin with increasing farm production, since so many LDC citizens live in the countryside and are dependent upon agriculture for their employment. Paradoxically, therefore, agricultural success in the South tends in the long run to be associated with larger rather than smaller agricultural imports. See Robert L. Paarlberg, "United States Agriculture and the Developing World: Partners or Competitors?" Final Report of an Agricultural Policy Study by the Curry Foundation, Washington, 1986.
3. "Latin Debt: A Global Impact," *Farmline*, vol. 7, no. 10 (October 1986), p. 8.
4. James A. Baker III, Statement before the Joint Annual Meeting of the World Bank and the International Monetary Fund, Seoul, South Korea, October 8, 1985.
5. Bruce Cumings, "The Origins and Development of the Northeast Asian Political Economy," *International Organization*, vol. 38, no. 1 (Winter 1984), p. 24.
6. World Bank, *World Development Report 1986, op. cit.*, p. 218.

Appendix

The Steering Committee
The Council on Foreign Relations
International Trade Project

Edmund T. Pratt, Jr., *Chairman*
C. Michael Aho, *Director of Project*
Suzanne H. Hooper, *Assistant Director of Project*

Thomas O. Bayard
C. Fred Bergsten
Senator Bill Bradley
William H. Branson
Sol Chick Chaikin
Lindley Clark
Ann Crittenden
June V. Cross
William Diebold, Jr.
William D. Eberle
Geza Feketekuty
Martin S. Feldstein
Murray H. Finley
Orville L. Freeman
Richard N. Gardner
Victor Gotbaum
Joseph A. Greenwald

Irene W. Meister
George R. Melloan
Ruben F. Mettler
John R. Opel
Sylvia Ostry
William R. Pearce
John R. Petty
Richard R. Rivers
Felix G. Rohatyn
Howard D. Samuel
Daniel A. Sharp
Ronald Shelp
Leonard Silk
Joan E. Spero
Helena Stalson
John J. Stremlau
William N. Walker

Catherine Gwin
Robert D. Hormats
Gary C. Hufbauer
John H. Jackson
Abraham Katz
Paul H. Kreisberg
Harald B. Malmgren

Marina v.N. Whitman
Lynn R. Williams
Alan W. Wolff
Lewis H. Young
John Zysman

Peter Tarnoff, *ex officio*

Members
The Study Group on The Future of U.S. Agricultural Trade Policy

Joseph A. Greenwald, *Study Group Chairman*
Robert L. Paarlberg, *Study Group Director*

Graham Avery
Kenneth Bader
Atherton Bean
Robert Bergland
Donald B. Billings
Senator Rudy Boschwitz
Carter Brandon
Cheryl Christensen
Richard N. Cooper
I.M. Destler
William Diebold, Jr.
Orville L. Freeman
Paul Fribourg
Catherine Gwin
Carol Rae Hansen
Ann L. Hollick
Barbara Insel
Jerome Jacobson
Timothy Josling
Abraham Katz
Julius Katz
Ulrich Koester
John Mellor
Donald Nelson

William R. Pearce
Dan Pearson
Gerald A. Pollack
Roger Porter
Derwent Renshaw
George Rossmiller
C. Ford Runge
Herbert Salzman
Fred Sanderson
Tom Saylor
J. Robert Schaetzel
John A. Schnittker
Ed Schuh
Helena Stalson
David H. Swanson
Stephan Tangermann
Paul Thompson
Robert L. Thompson
Luther Tweeten
Donna U. Vogt
Harald Von Wintzke
P.A.J. Wijnmaalen
Maurice J. Williams

Glossary Of Acronyms and Abbreviations

ASP	American Selling Price
CAP	Common Agricultural Policy of the European Community
CCC	Commodity Credit Corporation
CRP	Conservation Reserve Program
CSE	Consumer subsidy equivalent
CTA	GATT Committee on Trade in Agriculture
EAGGF	European Agricultural Guidance and Guarantee Fund
EEP	Export-Enhancement Program
EC	European Community
ECU	European Currency Unit
FAO	United Nations Food and Agriculture Organization
GATT	General Agreement on Tariffs and Trade
GDP	Gross Domestic Product
GNP	Gross National Product
HFCS	High fructose corn syrup
ICA	International commodity agreement
IMF	International Monetary Fund
IWA	International Wheat Agreement
IWC	International Wheat Council (London)
IIASA	International Institute of Applied Systems Analysis (Austria)
ITC	United States International Trade Commission
ITO	International Trade Organization

LDC	Less Developed Country
NTB	Nontariff barrier
OECD	Organization for Economic Cooperation and Development
OPEC	Organization of Petroleum Exporting Countries
PIE	Producer-incentive equivalent
PIK	Payment in Kind
PSE	Producer-subsidy equivalent
TEA	Targeted Export Assistance
UNCTAD	United Nations Conference on Trade and Development
USDA	United States Department of Agriculture
VAT	Value-Added Tax

Index

About the Author

Since 1976, *Robert L. Paarlberg* has been an Associate Professor of political science at Wellesley College and an Associate at the Harvard Center for International Affairs. He holds a Ph.D from Harvard University (1975) and an undergraduate degree from Carleton College (1967). He has also served as a Lieutenant in the U.S. Naval Reserve and as a legislative aide in the U.S. Senate. Paarlberg has received research grants to study international agricultural policy from the Ford and Rockefeller Foundations and the National Center for Food and Agricultural Policy at Resources for the Future. His recent publications include *Food Trade and Foreign Policy* (Cornell University Press, 1985); *Food in the Global Arena*, with R. Hopkins and M. Wallerstein (Holt, Rinehart and Winston, 1982); and "United States Agriculture and the Developing World: Partners or Competitors?" (A Report for the Curry Foundation, 1986). Dr. Paarlberg is currently researching the problem of agriculture reform.